Nonprofit Board

ANSWER BOOK

Practical Guide for Board Members and Chief Executives

EXPANDED EDITION

Robert C. Andringa

Ted W. Engstrom

BOARDSOURCE

Building Effective Nonprofit Boards

Formerly the National Center for Nonprofit Boards

BOARDSOURCE
Building Effective Nonprofit Boards

© 2002 BoardSource
ISBN: 1-58686-029-1
Printed in the United States of America

BoardSource
Suite 900
1828 L Street, NW
Washington, DC 20036-5104

Tel. 202-452-6262
Fax 202-452-6299
e-mail boardsource@boardsource.org
www.boardsource.org

Library of Congress Cataloging-in-Publication Data

Andringa, Robert C.
      Nonprofit board answer book: practical guidelines for board members and chief
executives/ by Robert C. Andringa and Ted W. Engstrom.—2nd ed., new and expanded ed.
        p.cm.
      Includes bibliographical references and index.
      ISBN 1-58686-029-1
      1. Nonprofit organizations—Management. 2. Directors of corporations. I. Engstrom,
Theodore Wilhelm, 1916- II. Title.

  HD62.6.A53 2001
  658.4'22—dc21

                                                                                    2001052422

Contents

Acknowledgments

Expertise on board development comes mostly by interaction with all kinds of boards. Books and tapes are useful, but principles of excellence are discovered mainly through the trial and error of real-life governance.

Whatever good principles we are adding to the literature in this venture must be attributed to the hundreds of nonprofit boards with which we have worked. Many good experiences have come from serving on a wide range of boards. Other insights have come from consultations with boards, both good ones and those still learning. To all of them, we are forever indebted. Translating these experiences into a common-sense book of practical advice has been both delightful and trying.

The original edition of the *Nonprofit Board Answer Book* was immensely popular. Much of the information from that volume has been included in this new edition, which addresses more of the questions we and the staff at BoardSource (formerly the National Center for Nonprofit Boards) hear in our work with boards.

There would be no expanded edition without the kind invitation of Janis Johnston, former publications director at BoardSource (formerly the National Center for Nonprofit Boards). That was the highest kind of compliment for an author. Special thanks go to Outi Flynn, the very capable responder to all manner of questions people ask of the Board Information Center at BoardSource. Outi's thorough, disciplined approach to governance and her quick return of first drafts with suggestions and edits provided the incentive to keep writing.

No author sees a final product without the encouragement, ideas, constructive feedback and fresh perspectives of many others. In addition to Janis and Outi, we want to thank Karen Colburn, who succeeded Janis in managing the project, and BoardSource Group Directors Kathleen Enright and Sharon Cumby Fay for their insightful direction. To the extent our conversational style flows in readable form, the credit goes to Ellen Hirzy who edited the manuscript. Seven chapters benefited from the careful review of Chip Grange and Rick Scanpanelli of Gammon & Grange, P.C., two of the country's most skilled and dedicated attorneys in nonprofit law. There were other reviewers, senior staff, designers, and proofreaders whose competencies added to what you have in your hands. To all we are very grateful.

We cannot say enough about the encouragement and patience we received from our spouses, Susan Andringa and Dorothy Engstrom. Each has been a gift from God in this and all endeavors to add value to the sector we love, the nonprofit world.

Their support was complemented by several other "encourager couples" in the process — the Laughlins, Lefevers, Knubels, McBrides, Stevensons, Cryers, Crawfords, and Lows. Thanks also go to two executive assistants at the Council for Christian Colleges and Universities, Jennifer Jukanovich and Maye Saephan, along with CCCU's outstanding board and colleagues Rich Gathro, Ron Mahurin, Kyle Royer, and Kevin Trowbridge.

Finally, we must thank the founders and leaders of BoardSource (formerly the National Center for Nonprofit Boards). There is no single catalyst for nonprofit governance in the world that can compare. We would not be as informed, experienced, confident — or published — without their vision and commitment.

Robert C. Andringa
Vienna, Virginia

Ted W. Engstrom
Pasadena, California

Foreword

Behind every good answer
lies a good question.

Good questions were the genesis not only of the *Nonprofit Board Answer Book*, but also of BoardSource, formerly the National Center for Nonprofit Boards. Thousands of hard-working, committed individuals who serve on boards or staffs of nonprofits, asking tough questions about governance were the impetus behind the creation of NCNB. Now, another generation of nonprofit leaders has helped us discover new ways in which we can serve nonprofits with smart, innovative solutions to governance problems as we have developed our new identity — BoardSource.

When we opened more than a decade ago with three staff members, we diligently tried to answer all the questions that came in from nonprofit chief executives across the country. As awareness of the importance of governance increased, the number of questions grew dramatically, and continues to do so. One way we meet this demand for specialized solutions is through our Board Information Center, a department dedicated entirely to answering these questions on an individual basis. Outi Flynn, manager of the Board Information Center, provided essential insights into the revision of this book by sharing with Bob Andringa and Ted Engstrom her wisdom about the most pressing governance issues on people's minds.

The nonprofit sector continues to transform itself to meet society's needs. We understand how important boards are for building strong communities. To make the transition from the National Center for Nonprofit Boards to BoardSource, we posed many of the questions in this book to a wide variety of nonprofit board and staff members who care about governance. We found out what kinds of challenges they're facing, and what they needed in terms of governance solutions. That's why we decided to offer a revised and expanded version of the *Nonprofit Board Answer Book*. This version provides nonprofit leaders with an improved resource with even more of the creative and practical solutions they need about essential topics and emerging issues in the sector. We've included 25 new chapters on such topics as transforming board and committee structure to improve meetings, how the board can best find and work with the chief executive, and the board's critical role in financial oversight.

With decades of experience working with hundreds of organizations, Bob Andringa and Ted Engstrom bring an impressive breadth and depth of knowledge about boards to the *Nonprofit Board Answer Book*. We thank them, and we thank Outi Flynn, for their dedication and insights. We are confident this volume will prove useful to new and seasoned nonprofit leaders around the world. Of course, new questions will continue to emerge, and we encourage you to ask them.

Judith O'Connor
President and CEO, BoardSource

Introduction

Without consultation, plans are frustrated,
but with many counselors they succeed.
A man has joy in an apt answer,
and how delightful is a timely word.
—Proverbs 15:22-23

A few days before Nebraska beat Florida for the 1996 college football national championship, Cornhuskers receivers' coach Ron Brown contrasted two types of players he sees every day. One type has turned Nebraska into a perennial contender, he pointed out. The other rarely sees action. "As a coach," Brown said, "I'm not interested in 'part-time' players. Over the course of a long season, part-time players will let you down—*guaranteed!* I'm looking for full-time players who will show up ready to play every day, every play."

This expanded edition of the *Nonprofit Board Answer Book* is for committed members of nonprofit boards and their chief executives—the full-time players who desire an "apt answer" and a "timely word" as they meet head-on the leadership challenges in the growing independent sector. Answering 60 of the questions most frequently asked by nonprofit board members and chief executives, this new and expanded edition offers comprehensive coverage of nonprofit governance.

Nonprofit organizations are one of America's greatest heritages and a distinguishing feature of our society. Business supplies goods and services, government controls and regulations, but the nonprofit organization has a different mission. Its "product," writes Peter F. Drucker,[1] "is neither a pair of shoes nor an effective regulation. Its product is a changed human being. The nonprofit institutions are human-change agents." We are drawn to what Drucker calls the "high ground effort of changing lives for the better" in a world of selfish interests.

Changing lives is heady business, and working with people of similar goals is a pleasure. But it is also a challenge. The agenda is usually open-ended and subject to change at any moment. You must please many constituencies, often with differing priorities. Much of your success depends on raising enough funds and finding enough good volunteers. The measurement of results is difficult and open to various interpretations. The days are as long as they are in any professional job.

We've worked closely with leaders in government and business, and it is clear: the board and chief executive of a nonprofit organization typically have a greater leadership challenge than their for-profit or government counterparts.

Consider this book a friendly conversation between us, because we would like to help you meet that challenge. Most of our insights apply to all nonprofits, even across national borders. Adopt the principles that apply to your situation, but enjoy the freedom to be an exception when that works for you. The aim is not to impress you with new theories or fancy rhetoric; it is to motivate you to meet challenges with positive action. Use the "Suggested Action Steps" at the close of each chapter to involve your colleagues in dialogue that can make your board more effective.

---

1. Peter F. Drucker, *Managing the Nonprofit Organization* (New York: HarperCollins, 1990), p. xiv.

Part I

Board Functions

What are the attributes of
a quality board?

"I just need to see the big picture of what a good board is."

Providing excellent governance to the organizations they serve is every board's goal, but often boards are too mired in the work of governance to stand back and see the big picture. These ten principles of good practice, listed briefly here, are discussed throughout the *Answer Book*. These attributes don't guarantee success, but boards can't get there without them.

I. The role of the board is clear and distinct from the role of staff.

As volunteers elected to serve a group function, a board's primary role is governance. The staff's primary role is management. Conflict emerges when either side views the other as competing for some of its rightful authority. Of course, the line between governance and management can be fuzzy and may often seem to overlap. But the best paradigm for smooth relationships is to see these two important roles as parallel and noncompeting.

It may help to think of board members as representing the "moral owners" (some would say stakeholders). When the board is clear about its role, there is less micromanagement and less confusion for both board and staff.

2. Board members understand their "three hats" — governance hat, volunteer hat, and policy implementer hat.

Imagine three baseball caps, only one of which can be worn at any given time. These are the three main roles a board member can play. Good boards and staffs understand when each role is appropriate. The primary hat — the governance hat — is worn only during legally-convened board meetings.

3. The board is clear about its moral owners (those to whom it feels accountable) and is clear about the organization's primary beneficiaries.

These concepts, introduced by John Carver,[1] help boards to distinguish between the people who are stakeholders (e.g., members, donors, and alumni) and those the organization serves.

In some nonprofits, the moral owners are the same as the primary beneficiaries. In trade associations, for example, the board is morally accountable to the members who pay dues, but the association's work is also focused on serving the same group.

In other organizations, the primary beneficiaries might be clearly defined, but the board may need to discuss to whom it should be accountable. Once defined, the board should find ways to solicit input from these moral owners and periodically report to them on their board work.

4. The board adopts clear ends policies.

Boards often struggle with adding specificity to their goals. Ends policies must clearly delineate what benefits or services will be offered, to whom, and at what cost or priority to the organization.

Here is an example: "We will provide conferences for communications directors in health-related nonprofit organizations and, through registration

fees, contribute a 10 percent net return to the general operating budget."
This makes clear that conferences are to be profit-making — not subsidized
— activities.

Here's another ends policy a board could adopt: "We will provide a service
to the elderly in our county through the production of video training
tapes as long as grant funds are available to cover the entire cost,
including staff time."

**5. The chief executive is responsible for achieving goals within clear board
parameters.**

Some nonprofit boards try to hire, evaluate, and oversee two or three
key people. It never works. The board needs one person — the chief executive
— to assume all responsibility and authority from the board. The lines of
accountability are clear and there are no excuses. The chief executive may
hire people to help and hold them accountable in a management system
that best fits the chief executive's style.

**6. All board standing policies are organized in one document, encompass
all board functions, and are reviewed frequently.**

Most boards react to specific issues or crises without the benefit of clear
policy guidelines. In fact, it is possible to capture every ongoing policy the
board will ever need in about 15 pages. This document should be reviewed
by committees and the board and continually modified as the board gathers
experience and wisdom. This paradigm of governance covers all policy bases
and frees staff to work within clearly defined guidelines between meetings.

7. The board chair manages the board with support from the chief executive.

Any team, even those made up of all-stars, needs a leader. The board
chair manages the board and the chief executive manages the organization.
Research shows that good boards have board-oriented chief executives.
When the chair and the chief executive stick to their roles and provide mutual
support to one another, the whole organization works better.

8. Committees are formed to efficiently serve the board's needs, not staff needs, and should speak to the board, not for it. Staff can help committees fulfill that role.

Committees are useful only when they help the board do its work better. Once formed, they should work to formulate good recommendations for board action. They don't replace the board's authority. Good staff know their job is to help committees do board work, not staff work. Too often staff develop committee agendas that address their own management issues rather than the issues necessary to formulate sound recommendations for the board.

Task forces, which are designed for a specific purpose and then dissolved after the mission is accomplished, may offer an efficient alternative to committees.

9. Board meetings are well planned with board-friendly advance materials, good agendas, clear results, and time for board fellowship.

Most board members evaluate whether to stay on a board by reflecting on the quality of meetings. Many board meetings are tedious. Many are much ado about nothing. Busy board members may question their importance.

Advance preparation can make board meetings productive and enjoyable. Board members like to go home feeling that they set important policy to advance the mission. Remember — great boards have memorable meetings.

10.Board members are selected based on careful consideration to board composition, are well oriented both before and right after election, and are regularly trained.

Any team that wants to win the championship takes care to select, orient, and train its members. In football, having three great quarterbacks and no receivers would be ludicrous. But some boards have never defined the profile of their own "dream team" and then worked deliberately to find people with the motivations, values, experience, and skills to help the organization reach new levels of excellence. As for orientation, good boards do some of it prior to elections so candidates are not surprised or disappointed when they begin their jobs. But post-election orientation and ongoing board training is even more important.

No matter how professional the staff is, good boards are essential to organizational success. And it is imperative that boards assume responsibility for their own evaluation and strategies for improvement.

SUGGESTED ACTION STEPS

1. Distribute these attributes for discussion at your next board meeting.

2. Ask an informed volunteer to come and watch a full board meeting, sit in on a few committee meetings, and then give you an honest assessment based on these ten attributes of quality.

3. Challenge each board member to come up with a personal list of 10 indicators of success for your board.

---

1. John Carver, *Boards that Make a Difference*, 2nd ed. (San Francisco, CA: Jossey-Bass, 1997).

2

What are the fundamental roles of a nonprofit board?

*"My greatest concern is that our board
gets too involved in administration."*

Discovering a clear role brings energy and freedom to individuals as well as organizations. If you could observe the board meetings of hundreds of nonprofit groups, as we have, you would be struck by their diversity. Boards can range in size from three to more than 100 people. Their structure, strength of leadership, working style, and relationship with staff varies almost as much.

Just as boards themselves are inherently diverse, so are the assumptions individual board members bring to the group. For this reason, a shared understanding of the roles of a nonprofit board is essential to effective governance. One of the best lists of board functions is found in *Ten Basic Responsibilities of Nonprofit Boards*, published by BoardSource (formerly the National Center for Nonprofit Boards).[1] Use these 10 functions as a checklist for clarifying your board's role:

1. Determine the organization's mission and purposes.

2. Select the chief executive.
3. Support the chief executive and assess his or her performance.
4. Ensure effective organizational planning.
5. Ensure adequate resources.
6. Manage resources effectively.
7. Determine, monitor, and strengthen the organization's programs and services.
8. Enhance the organization's public standing.
9. Ensure legal and ethical integrity and maintain accountability.
10. Recruit and orient new board members and assess board performance.

Is each function being carried out in your organization, either by the full board or by the chief executive as delegated by the board? Does your board do more? If so, does its expanded role make sense?

Here is another framework for clarifying role definitions. Think of each board member as having three hats to wear:

1. *Governance hat:* Worn only when the full board meets, proper notice has been given, and a quorum is present.
2. *Implementation hat:* Worn only when the board gives one or more board members authority to implement a board policy.
3. *Volunteer hat:* Worn at all other times, when board members are involved with organizational activities as volunteers.

Problems arise when board members or staff confuse these hats or when board members assume that *individual* and *collective* board responsibilities are interchangeable. They are not. Much of the confusion has to do with authority. Here is how we distinguish the three hats for individual board members:

- *Governance hat.* The board is the ultimate legal and moral authority for the nonprofit corporation. The government authorizes the board to be accountable to the public for running the corporation. An *individual* board member has no authority in governance. Governance is *group* action.

- *Implementation hat.* Occasionally the board delegates authority to at least one of its members to act on its behalf — to negotiate the purchase of a van, for example, or to determine which firm will do the next financial audit. Such authority is not automatic just because a person is a board member. It depends on the board having given its authority, acting by resolution in an official meeting.

- *Volunteer hat.* When serving as a volunteer, board members are accountable to someone else within the organization, whether the chief executive, the volunteer coordinator, another staff member, or a task force chair.

The most misunderstood and abused principle of governance is the requirement for group action. The chief executive and staff cannot serve two (or 22) masters. The full board sets policy, not individual board members. Board members and staff need to be reminded of this principle. Otherwise, confusion and conflict reign and board effectiveness is diminished.

In most organizations, the board looks to the staff to implement its policy. The same standard applies to tasks the board assigns to one of its members. When wearing their implementation hats, board members act as staff would — they fulfill the task according to board policy and do not attempt to revise the policy or create a new one.

Small nonprofit organizations with few staff often have board members who can jump in to help with details. Most depend heavily on board members to set up luncheons, enlist other volunteers, raise funds, help stuff envelopes, put up banners, write newsletter articles, and more. But in this role, board members are volunteering to help the chief executive and staff complete tasks that fulfill the organization's mission. During these volunteer hours, board members must not try to run the program simply because they are board members.

The concept of these three hats — governance, implementation, and volunteer — is not understood automatically. The board needs to discuss how its roles differ from those of the staff, agree on a model that fits the organization, and orient both board and staff to their distinctive roles. Then the board is much less likely to become involved inappropriately in administration.

SUGGESTED ACTION STEPS

1. Determine where you are. Give each board member a blank sheet of paper and ask each to write what she or he believes the role of the board to be. Consolidate the responses in a summary report for discussion at the next meeting. Try to reach consensus on the distinction between board and staff roles.

2. Ask a friendly but knowledgeable and objective volunteer to read the board's minutes from the past year and then observe two board meetings. Ask this person to summarize on one page what the board role is (not what someone says it *should* be). You'll find out quickly whether or not you are walking the talk.

---

1. Richard T. Ingram, *Ten Basic Responsibilities of Nonprofit Boards,* rev. ed. (Washington, DC: National Center for Nonprofit Boards [now BoardSource], 1997).

3

What are the major differences between nonprofit and for-profit boards?

"In the corporation I serve, senior paid executives have the strongest role on our board."

Many nonprofit board members are more familiar with the corporate world than with the nonprofit world. They often suggest, "Why don't we do it the way a good corporation does?"

There are fundamental differences between these two types of corporate boards (a nonprofit organization is an incorporated entity, too). The differences are in purpose, effectiveness, and motivation, not so much in legal principles. The information in Figure 1 can be useful to stimulate discussion among your board members.

We do not mean to say that nonprofit boards have nothing to learn from their for-profit counterparts. Both situations provide good experience in group discussion and consensus building. Both need strong board chairs who bring

Figure I

Profit vs. Nonprofit Boards

	PROFIT	NONPROFIT
Overarching goal	Generate profits for owners/ shareholders	Change lives by fulfilling a mission of service to its constituency
Size	Relatively small (three to seven)	Median size of 17, but often quite large (as many as 40 or 50)
Membership	Primary owners, business, executives or other professionals	Variety of people from business, government, and voluntary sectors
Term of office	Often no term limits	Many have term limits
Moral owners	Shareholders	The public, association members, donors, church, or others
Primary beneficiaries	Owners, through profits	Recipients of services as defined in mission
Board elections	By shareholders according to shares owned	By a variety of peer board members, appointed by another authority, or a combination
Compensation	The majority are paid	Most are not paid
Staff	Almost always paid, often according to performance	Paid and unpaid staff
Public accountability	Very private, disclosing only what law requires	Extensive, frequently providing reports and making activities widely known

out the best in the board members. Both have the potential to use committees for informed decision making.

But the differences are as important as the similarities. For example, we believe the only staff member who should even be considered for a nonprofit board position is the chief executive, and then only as an *ex officio* member without vote (see Chapter 38). In a for-profit corporation, several paid executives typically serve on the board, and sometimes they form a majority. The chief executive usually chairs the board, a situation we feel is less than ideal for reasons of accountability in the nonprofit sector. As you will see in later chapters, we believe the role of the board is separate from, and not in competition with, the role of the chief executive.

SUGGESTED ACTION STEPS

1. Take 10 minutes in a board meeting to brainstorm the differences between nonprofit and for-profit boards. Let board members identify the differences that are important to them.

2. Then show participants Figure 1. Find out whether they agree, and identify other distinctions related to your situation.

4

Do small boards operate differently from large boards?

"We're such a small board that most board principles don't apply to us."

The answer is... not much. The job description for a governing board is the same regardless of board size. Most of the differences in how boards function are related more to other variables than to the size of the board.

The culture of the organization, leadership style of the chair, support from the chief executive, nature of the mission, experience of board members, number of meetings, and similar variables all have a stronger impact on the way a board functions than size. There are some notable differences, however, between small and large boards:

- Scheduling meetings and getting a quorum may be easier with small boards, especially if all board members live close by. A board of five can look ahead at calendars and agree to meet only when all members are available. That is much harder to do with a board of 30.

- Friendships among board members and knowledge of, and dependence on, one another's strengths is often a distinction of smaller boards. There can be a greater sense of being needed and therefore a higher level of motivation for participating fully on a smaller board.

- Identifying and recruiting new board members is less time consuming on smaller boards. The flip side to this, however, is that a small board may recruit only those well known to the members. Larger boards are often better at recruiting board members who reflect the diversity necessary to fulfill the mission.

- Orientation of new board members, if done well both before and after members are elected, takes more time with large boards.

- Small boards may govern less formally. Larger boards may be more disciplined about establishing written policies and procedures.

- The chief executive officer and key staff may find it easier to stay in close communication with and learn what motivates board members if the board has fewer members. This also makes the chair's job of managing the board a bit easier.

- Since many nonprofits depend on more volunteers than could ever be on the board, a large board does not necessarily change how the program staff operate. Yet, board members can be effective in fund-raising and community outreach, so a large board provides more informed leaders for these key volunteer hat roles. But remember — the main reason we focus on building good boards is for governance, not more volunteers.

- While small boards may have greater cohesion among members, they also run the risk of burnout if expectations are high. There are fewer people to share the load.

- Finally, there is one big difference in how small and large boards function: Most small boards can govern well without committees. Committees of large boards can be just as much a hindrance to good governance as an asset; it depends on how well they function.

While not related much to how boards operate, the cost of sustaining larger boards, especially when the organization offers to pay travel expenses, can be substantially higher. Another financial difference between large and small boards is the good practice of expecting each board member to donate annually. This could easily offset the extra cost of maintaining a larger board.

In summary, the differences in how boards function based on size alone are not that significant. The governance task is the same. How the job gets done, however, may vary as a result of board size. The points listed here may be helpful in evaluating whether resizing your board would make the organization more effective. Regardless of board size, the key for any board is to be committed to do the job well.

SUGGESTED ACTION STEPS

1. Make a list of how you think your board would function differently if it were half the size. How about twice the size?

2. Discuss possible reasons for your board's inefficiency other than its size.

5

How does the board sort out its role in relation to the staff?

"To be honest with you, our staff is so effective we could accomplish more without a board."

Too many chief executives seem to compete with their boards, so they have little motivation to help them define a clear, strong role. This situation is unfortunate because everyone can be more productive when roles are clear and board members and staff are not trying to do one another's work.

Have you ever experienced this scenario? Board members show up at the office and pitch in to get the work done. They often build strong friendships with staff. At board meetings, members, and staff sit around a table and discuss what to do. The board feels less informed than the staff and often inadequate, so it welcomes strong staff participation. Staff don't wait to be asked a question, but jump into the conversation whenever they have a point to make. Formal votes are seldom taken because the chair looks at the whole group and suggests: "We seem to have a consensus to move ahead as Tom suggested."

19

How does the board sort out its role in relation to the staff?

An observer of this organization would have a hard time figuring out how board and staff roles differ. But if people are served, morale is high, and the bills are getting paid, why worry about loose organizational style? One good reason is legal liability in organizations whose boards do not set and carefully document policy. But the most compelling reasons have to do with organizational effectiveness. In our experience, it is universally true that strong nonprofits have strong boards, and strong boards become excellent with the help of their organizations' chief executives. The best boards stick to their governance role and stay out of staff responsibilities when doing board work.

Even in the smallest, most informal organizations, it is possible for board and staff to learn when to put on and take off the three hats we described in Chapter 2. When the governance hat is called for in a duly assembled business meeting of the board and a quorum is present, the board should follow clearly defined roles and responsibilities. Some formality is both legally and practically appropriate.

We created the following simple comparison using the distinctions Cyril O. Houle makes between the board and the chief executive:[1]

Figure 2
Board vs. Chief Executive Role

THE BOARD	THE CHIEF EXECUTIVE
Is corporate; acts as a group	Is individual
Is continuous	Is temporary
Is part-time	Is full-time
Has no staff or minimal staff	Has access to all staff
Has ultimate responsibility	Has limited, immediate responsibility
Is typically not expert in the work of the organization	Is typically professional and an expert in this arena
Gives volunteer time	Earns a salary
Sees only parts of the whole	Is intimately involved in everything

Conflicts arise when staff are equipped to do a better job than a poorly functioning board. When it's time for the board to select new members, for example, staff frequently have greater knowledge of interested volunteers who might qualify for board membership. Staff sometimes also know more about the constituents served, the budget, and the workings of similar organizations.

In the business of sorting out roles, here is one principle most could agree with: Put it in writing. Oral tradition does not work well in nonprofit governance. Turnover of board members and staff can lead to confusion. Besides, people bring different experiences to the board room and translate them into different assumptions about what should happen. The result: miscommunication, misunderstandings, and mistakes.

The best approach is to think ahead and give clear signals about what the board intends to do and what it expects the staff to do. Decide together what works for the organization, within the board roles discussed in Chapter 2, and then write it down in simple and straightforward terms so the people involved, now and in the future, can easily refer to a written set of expectations. (See Chapter 15 for more on this principle.)

A good way to sort out board and staff roles is to put all the areas of confusion on the board table for open discussion. Invite board and staff to engage in a dialogue about this issue. The worksheet in Figure 3 may be useful in clarifying who does what.

You can see from this worksheet that there are more ways than one to accomplish an organization's work. We have found that a good paradigm for board-staff roles is John Carver's Policy Governance® model, explained in his book *Boards that Make a Difference*.[2] He suggests that the board start with the broadest statements of policy, develop more specific policies from them, and then at some point tell the staff: "We have said enough. Now you go ahead and make decisions that you feel are best. Just stay within the parameters we have defined for you and give us the reports we have asked for so we can monitor whether these policies are indeed the best ones for our organization." This is simple advice, but it works.

21

How does the board sort out its role in relation to the staff?

Figure 3

Board and Staff Roles Worksheet

FOR EACH ISSUE OR TASK, INDICATE WITH THE APPROPRIATE LETTER WHERE YOUR BOARD IS NOW AND WHERE IT SHOULD BE

A. Board initiates and decides on its own (chief executive may implement).

B. Chief executive formally recommends and board decides.

C. Chief executive decides and/or acts after consultation with board members during or outside of normal board or committee meetings.

D. Chief executive and/or staff act on their own within previous board policies.

ISSUES AND TASKS	IS NOW	SHOULD BE
1. Mission statement for organization		
2. Formal annual goals and objectives		
3. Recruitment of new board members		
4. Board and committee structure		
5. Policies regarding board role and activities		
6. Hiring and salaries of staff other than chief executive		
7. Changes in bylaws to keep current		
8. Annual income and expense budget		
9. Budget amendments as required		
10. Capital expenditures		
11. Staff compensation policies		
12. Other personnel policies and practices		
13. Investment policies		
14. Arrangements for external audit		
15. Fund-raising plan and policies		
16. Adoption of new programs or services		
17. Termination of current programs or services		
18. Staff organizational structure		
19. Organization's insurance program		
20. Board meeting agendas		
21. Other:		

✓ SUGGESTED ACTION STEPS

1. Ask each board member to submit a list of areas in which board-staff roles are unclear.

2. Use a worksheet similar to the one in this chapter to stimulate dialogue and agreement.

3. If you are too close to your forest to see the trees, invite a board mentor to come in to observe a couple of board meetings (see Chapter 53) and staff meetings. Then ask for honest feedback on where clarification is needed.

---

1. Cyril O. Houle, *Governing Boards: Their Nature and Nurture* (San Francisco, CA: Jossey-Bass, 1989).

2. John Carver, *Boards that Make a Difference*, 2nd ed. (San Francisco, CA: Jossey-Bass, 1997).

6

What is the board's role in determining mission and strategic planning?

*"Are we heading toward the place
we eventually want to be?"*

Few things frustrate board members more than fuzzy thinking about where an organization is heading. It can be a free-for-all, with board committees and senior staff all following different paths.

A board must ask continually: What is our purpose? Who are we serving? How are we doing? Where are we going? Strategic planning is a way to sort out these questions. But make no mistake: Strategic planning is difficult. It requires time, resources, patience, conflict resolution, persistence, and controversial choices. Most view strategic planning as the complicated, laborious task of producing a long document that often gets put on a shelf and has little impact. But planning is not just a product. It is a process that demands the full attention and involvement of the board.

GET THE MISSION FIRST

"Mission is everything," a friend observed. Until there is not only consensus but some passion about a clear mission, strategic planning can be a waste of time. Mission is the reason you exist as an organization. Would the world lack anything if someone didn't achieve your mission? How do you know whether to add or eliminate a program unless you can link it to your mission?

In addition to stating a clear mission, some people like to identify a vision, principles, corporate values, and other organizational goals. All of these can be good, and we don't believe everyone needs to have the same definitions. Generally, we think of a vision statement as a long-term achievement that will involve more than your own organization. A mission statement is the change (often in specific people's lives) that your organization intends to accomplish. From the mission flow specific goals and objectives in the strategic plan.

We prefer mission statements of fewer than 25 to 30 words so they can be easily printed and literally memorized by board members, staff, and others. Some organizations even use three or four key words on their letterheads. A good mission statement is whatever helps one focus his or her thinking and actions on what distinguishes your organization from others. It should not so much describe the organization as define the results it seeks to achieve.

Achieving consensus on a mission statement can be difficult, but it is an essential exercise and should be put on the board's agenda at least once a year. The chief executive should be asked to do reports tied to the mission statement. That means the mission should be measurable to some extent. While mission is not usually changed every year, we do live in an environment where new laws, dramatic economic or environmental shifts, other organizations entering the picture, or other changes can justify a revision.

We hope we are stating the obvious: Without a clear mission statement, good strategic planning is impossible. Strategic planning — and ongoing strategic thinking — must be linked to your organization's purpose.

THE PLANNING PROCESS

There are many good books about the strategic planning process, but how to get the job done is less important than achieving the desired results. Guy S. Saffold, a university administrator, expresses much of our thinking in his insightful and practical book, *Strategic Planning for Christian Organizations*. These observations help stimulate careful thinking about strategic planning:

- Strategic planning is an attempt to let future priorities have an influence on today's activities.

- Strategic thinking is more important than strategic planning.

- Strategic planning has the potential to generate conflict, to waste time, and to consume resources for relatively little return.

- The goal of strategic planning is not to develop plans but to stimulate action.[1]

Another respected author on this topic is John M. Bryson, who warns about focusing on procedures rather than on strategic thinking: "If any particular approach to strategic planning gets in the way of strategic thought and action, the planning approach should be scrapped."[2]

MAKING THE CASE FOR PLANNING

The board's interest in strategic planning is to help the board do its work of governance and the staff to do its work of management. Boards reflect the whole spectrum, from delegating the job fully to the chief executive to setting up task forces and running the entire process. We believe the board has an important, albeit a limited, role.

First, the board needs to establish the "why" of strategic planning. Otherwise, the cost in time, money, and emotions is too high. Involve board members, staff, and perhaps key donors and friends in this discussion.

Here are some reasons we believe strategic planning is critical to any organization:

- *Survival.* There is no guarantee of survival, no matter how compelling a mission you have. When key players doubt the viability of an organization, the board must set in place a planning process to address the burning questions.

- *Achieving the mission.* Organizations tend to wander from their stated missions, taking on new programs and serving new constituencies because money is available or new leaders want to do different things. Sometimes the mission statement is indistinguishable from that of other organizations, or it may be seldom referred to in decision making. In today's world, it is crucial that board and staff stay focused on mission. Strategic planning helps that to happen.

- *Reality check.* Old methods may not meet the needs of today's environment. Drifting along, assuming that the problems of fund-raising, participation, or program quality will correct themselves, is a sure road to disaster. Strategic planning can identify new realities that must be addressed sooner rather than later.

- *Focus.* Even with a good mission statement and relative success, most organizations should periodically review which actions bring the most results, which old activities are no longer significant, and where the majority of resources should be directed.

- *Consensus and ownership.* It is not enough for the chief executive to have a clear picture of where the organization is going. The benefits of board, staff, and constituent consensus on strategic direction are obvious. Consensus requires good communication and periodic consultation with a variety of people about how well the organization is doing and what it should be doing next.

- *Effectiveness.* Some nonprofits are good at doing the wrong things. Effectiveness, Peter Drucker says, is "doing the right things." In a world of limited resources, choosing the best among the good is difficult and requires regular, conscious strategic thinking.

27

What is the board's role in determining mission and strategic planning?

- *Leadership review*. Being human, board members often hesitate to address the sensitive issue of whether and when a leadership change is needed for the challenges ahead. Organizations go through cycles, each handled best by a leader who fits the times. Strategic planning can help a board determine what the times require.

EMBRACING A PLAN

Once the rationale for strategic planning is clear, someone (usually the chief executive) should look at different models and present a proposal, especially if strategic planning has not been the regular pattern of organizational leadership. The proposal should have board approval and reflect at least the following items:

- *Who will lead the strategic planning process?* We generally like the chief executive to have this role, whether assisted by an outside consultant or not.

- *What is the time frame?* We think from six to nine months is most effective. The participants can wear out if the process drags on. Schedule interim reports to the board.

- *Who will be involved?* The process should include board, staff, major donors, key "moral owners" (the people to whom the board is accountable), perhaps community leaders, and others.

- *What is the budget?* The process need not be expensive, but there are some direct expenses if it is done well.

- *What are the expected outcomes?* Be specific about reports, how relative priorities are to be identified, and whatever else the leadership expects from the process.

Once the board reviews and approves the strategic planning proposal, the management of the planning process is usually delegated to the chief executive. However, some organizations, for good reasons, put a particularly gifted board member or even an outside consultant in charge. Board members then become involved according to their time and interests.

ADOPTING MAJOR GOALS AS POLICY

One product of strategic planning should be a fairly short list of major goals embraced by the board. John Carver calls these "ends" policies. He considers ends, results, and outcomes as the same thing. We like his definition of desired results as "what human needs are satisfied, for whom and at what cost."[3]

Remember this important point about approving a strategic plan: The plan the board formally adopts should consist of long-range, macro policies dealing with mission and results; it should not be a full-blown plan containing staff action steps that might need to be changed from time to time. The board should expect the planning process to generate specific goals, objectives, and action steps for the staff that go beyond the major board-approved goals.

ENCOURAGING STRATEGIC THINKING

A formal planning process will encourage strategic thinking by the organization's leadership. An extensive, months-long process with task forces, committees, and reports may not be required for another several years, but strategic thinking, learned and reinforced through the planning exercise, must become the mode of thinking about all aspects of the organization.

A board can underline its commitment to strategic thinking by requiring staff to provide certain monitoring data that track how well the desired results are being achieved. This requirement forces critical analysis and creative reflection about new ways to achieve outcomes, or it forces reconsideration of the stated outcomes.

Sometimes it is energizing and uplifting for staff and board to dream about what they would like to happen, without regard for cost, energy, or time. We once suggested to our senior staff that they develop, individually and as a group, five-year "dream sheets." Based on the information we gathered, we began to implement some of these "dreams." After five years, we found that 75 to 80 percent of what we had envisioned actually did happen because we applied our hearts and minds to fulfilling those dreams.

29

What is the board's role in determining mission and strategic planning?

A CONCLUDING THOUGHT

Strategic thinking is necessary, but don't let a sophisticated textbook process of strategic planning bog you down. Sometimes strategic thinking is spontaneous — an idea that comes to mind while you are driving to work, a thought written on a restaurant place mat. When the board is committed to an attitude of thinking strategically, new ideas that may seem disparate often come together in support of the mission and major goals of the organization. The benefits of a dynamic and flexible planning process will far outweigh the time, effort, and resources you invest.

SUGGESTED ACTION STEPS

1. If your organization has a strategic plan, help the board become more familiar with it.

2. Have a short discussion about other experiences board members have had with strategic planning and what approach might be best for your organization.

3. Brainstorm for an hour, listing the organization's strengths, weaknesses, opportunities, and threats. Find out how well the board responds to thinking strategically.

4. Develop a proposal for a formal strategic planning effort.

---

1. Guy S. Saffold, *Strategic Planning for Christian Organizations* (Fayetteville, AR: Accrediting Association of Bible Colleges, 1994).

2. John M. Bryson, *Strategic Planning for Public and Nonprofit Organizations* (San Francisco, CA: Jossey-Bass, 1988), p. 2.

3. John Carver, *Boards that Make a Difference*, 2nd ed. (San Francisco, CA: Jossey-Bass, 1997).

7

What is the board's role in fund-raising?

"When I was recruited for the board, no one mentioned I would have to give and get money."

Many boards expect members to make annual financial gifts appropriate to their means. They are expected to encourage others to give as well. Believe it or not, we know board members whose first love is raising money for the organizations they serve. In today's world, every board should have at least a few members who want to work with staff to generate contributions. Individuals in the United States give well over $100 billion to charities each year.[1] Your organization should get its fair share.

Remember that the board, as the corporate entity, holds ultimate responsibility for strategy, a capable staff, and adequate resources. Most organizations depend heavily on staff to assist the board in these functions, but the board cannot legally or morally opt out of any of them. Let's look at some specific roles of board members in fund-raising.

1. Give generously.

When board members show their personal commitment to give, others will follow suit. One useful rule of thumb is to expect every member, as a matter of policy, to be a "donor of record" every year — to have made a duly recorded contribution to the organization. Potential board members should know about this policy before they are elected to serve. During the year, the board should receive information on how much has been raised from the board and how many of its members have given to date. The amounts are not as important as the fact of giving. Foundations, government agencies, and individual donors will be impressed when your organization can report: "Every board member has donated this year."

Many boards require specific contributions as a condition of board service. We do not agree that *all* board members should be expected to be "heavy hitters," but it is fairly common for larger organizations to be honest with potential board members that giving or raising a certain amount each year is one of the expectations.

2. Approve plans and goals tied to the organization's mission.

The board that takes its responsibilities for mission seriously puts its organization in a stronger position to seek funds from outside sources. We discussed the board's role in defining and clarifying mission in Chapter 6. As part of its fund-raising responsibility, the board should pay close attention to the nature of the organization's mission and whether it needs review or revision. Fund-raising policies, plans, and goals should be tied closely to mission, and it is up to the board to make sure this happens.

3. Establish policies to guide fund-raising.

Written parameters, established by the board, should guide fund-raising. When creating policies, consider the following questions:

- Are there strategies the board *does not* want staff to pursue?
- What ethical standards should be followed?

- How much of the budget several years down the road should depend on outside giving?
- Does the board want to apply for government grants or contracts?
- What is the maximum percentage of the budget you want to spend on fund-raising?

Boards should not get carried away with details. Just provide wise direction for staff.

4. Select and encourage a development-savvy chief executive.

It is a given that chief executives spend a good deal of time raising money. But everyone needs help. Board members can pitch in with both time and advice. They can also encourage a chief executive to pursue education and training in this area. The board's affirmation of the chief executive — in fund-raising as well as in other areas — sends positive signals to staff and constituents and can often translate into fund-raising success.

5. Recruit a few board members willing to raise funds.

The network of contacts board members bring to an organization helps immensely in fund-raising. When designing a profile of the talents and experiences board members need, think of criteria that relate to this area. Be straightforward about recruiting prospective members you know will be especially effective. These rare people can do things even the best chief executive can seldom do.

6. Volunteer to help.

Every board member can volunteer a few hours to do what he or she does best and enjoys the most within the broad range of activities related to fund-raising. Offer many options, and let individual board members select one or two tasks. For example, board members might host a luncheon, sell tickets to an event, sign letters to people they know, and make follow-up thank-you calls to donors. Sometimes, board members who are not major donors are good at bringing enthusiastic support to the volunteer work that goes into reaching goals.

7. Evaluate your efforts.

Board members often represent a sample of the contributor profile, so they are in a good position to evaluate which fund-raising strategies work within a particular community and which ones do not. Staff members can be too close to the fund-raising process to evaluate the results objectively. Approaches that work well at first have a tendency to continue beyond their effectiveness. Regular informal evaluation helps prevent unfortunate situations like that of the organization that determined it was spending $75,000 each year in staff and materials to raise approximately $60,000 in its annual gifts campaign.

Most organizations have a few primary strategies for developing resources. The chart in Figure 4 shows many of the options. You might identify those that fit your organization and then invite each board member to select one, two, or three of the areas in which he or she would feel most comfortable assisting.

Figure 4

Sources and Types of Donations for Nonprofit Organizations

Identify which parts of this matrix fit your organization. Then ask each board member to circle at least three areas in which she or he feels most interested and able to help the organization in fund-raising.

SOURCE TYPE	INDIVIDUALS	BUSINESS	FOUNDATIONS	GOVERNMENT	OTHER NONPROFITS
Annual giving (unrestricted)	X	X	X	X	X
Direct mail (unrestricted)	X				
Project grants (unrestricted)	X	X	X	X	X
Events	X	X			
Capital gifts (buildings, endowment)	X	X	X	X	
Income from planned gifts	X				
In-kind (goods and services)	X	X			X
Approximate income in past two years	$_____	$_____	$_____	$_____	$_____

Adapted by Robert C. Andringa from Fisher Howe, *The Board Member's Guide to Fund-Raising* (San Francisco, CA: Jossey-Bass, 1991).

We hope you leave this chapter committed to the notion that every board member should be involved in generating resources. There is a productive role for everyone in fund-raising, and there is great satisfaction in contributing to the organization in this way. The question is: How can you develop a plan that makes the most of board and staff talents?

SUGGESTED ACTION STEPS

1. Consider having a staff presentation on current fund-raising efforts with an analysis of results and recommendations.

2. If you don't have one already, recommend a simple policy that says, "Each board member is expected to be a donor of record every year."

3. Ask the board's development committee to propose one page of policies, for board approval, designed to guide the organization's fund-raising efforts.

---

1. American Association of Fund-Raising Counsel, *Giving USA.*

8

How should the board communicate its activities to the broader community?

"To whom are we responsible, anyway?"

Every board should identify and define the "moral owners" of its organization: the people to whom the board should be accountable. Sometimes these people are called stakeholders. These identified groups are not always the same people as the primary beneficiaries of a nonprofit's work.[1] For example, in most membership organizations, the moral owners and the primary beneficiaries are the members. For a school board, the moral owners would usually be parents and taxpayers, while the primary beneficiaries are the students.

Effective boards form links with these constituencies. This is part of building loyalty and confidence in the organization's mission. Linking is a two-way street: The board listens to its constituencies, and it also communicates with them about the organization. Most boards depend on the staff for internal and external communication. They usually do not identify the board as a separate voice, preferring to speak on behalf of the whole organization. That is appropriate.

But why not encourage the board itself to be involved as the reporting entity to selected groups in the organization's constituency? And why not invite selected groups to communicate their ideas and concerns directly to the board?

Here are some examples to stimulate creative planning on how the reporting and listening roles might work. You may decide whether any of them fits your style and mission.

EXAMPLES OF BOARD REPORTING

1. A college board chair wrote to all donors about the school's participation in a matching program of a bankrupt foundation, assuring donors of the soundness of the college's finances and outlining how the institution intends to prevent similar problems in the future. Donors felt reassured by hearing from the board and learning of the school's mission rather than hearing from the staff, who probably solicited their donations in past fund-raising campaigns.

2. The entire board of a hospital involved in a merger signed a memorandum to patients, doctors, donors, and the media explaining the advantages of the merger and the process that was followed in making such an important decision. Since a board made this important decision, it was altogether appropriate for the decision makers to explain their actions directly to the various constituencies.

3. The chair of a mental health clinic sent a letter to the clinic's entire mailing list explaining the sudden termination of the chief executive and the plan for a transition until a new director could be found. Whenever there is a surprise change of leadership, the board should be the official source of information. The communication should be timely, forthright, courteous, and assuring.

4. The board of one agency approved a media release outlining the desired characteristics of a new chief executive being sought as a replacement. Again, any matter dealing with the chief executive is most appropriately communicated by the board.

5. The board of a major city arts organization decided donors would be attracted to its mission if its well-known chair were more visible. So they agreed she should write a column in every other newsletter and also write a signed letter for the opening page of the annual report. These are common, natural ways for the board to be viewed as actively engaged in the mission of the organization.

EXAMPLES OF BOARD LISTENING

1. Board members saw a major shift in the mission of their nonprofit agency as the potential for creating additional support. The board sent a survey to significant constituencies to get grassroots input. Because the survey came from the board, the recipients knew any major change to be announced later would be the result of serious deliberation.

2. A national association with thousands of members in each state decided to hold hearings in seven regions on how the association could improve its member services. At least three board members presided at each hearing along with the chief executive. This strategy showed the board's willingness to hear supporters' concerns and ideas, adding to their own credibility and to the credibility of the organization.

3. A drug prevention organization in a major city wanted to educate the community and give visibility to its mission. It decided to sponsor a local radio talk show, inviting callers to comment on various topics. Five board members prepared ahead of time and then co-hosted the shows with a local disk jockey who was interested in solving the drug problem.

4. A church's board of elders felt the congregation was so large that few people knew who the elders were and what they did. They organized

after-church brunches on 10 consecutive Sundays, inviting the congregation in alphabetical groupings. The elders made a brief presentation and responded to questions.

5. A public policy research center in Washington decided grassroots communication with a new Congress was more persuasive than simply writing and sending reports to the Hill. Six well-known scholars on the board agreed to write stimulating case studies outlining the pros and cons of key issues, putting them on the web so people around the world could comment. The board also encouraged participants to communicate directly with members of Congress who were highlighted in the documents.

6. A local rescue mission served approximately 500 homeless people in a year. In a board meeting, most members admitted they had never had a conversation of more than a minute or two with any of the men staying at the mission. The solution was to ask the mission director to bring two residents to each dinner that preceded board meetings so board members could listen to those they served. Their understanding of the mission's clientele rose dramatically.

In all of these examples, the board agreed how it would connect as a group with its constituents. The board chair, as the leader of the board, most often makes any public statements on behalf of the board, but other efforts to link with the community should be discussed and agreed upon by the board members.

The public profile of boards varies greatly. Some organizations achieve visibility and credibility mostly by having well-known people on the board. These organizations usually list board members' names on their letterheads and in their newsletters and other publications. We see no problem with that, but we are urging that even those boards consider a more overt means of connecting with the community.

Other boards prefer to keep a low profile. One major international organization prohibits board members from listing their board membership

39

How should the board communicate its activities to the broader community?

in their resumes or biographies. The intent is to promote the notion of leaders serving others and eliminate the temptation to use board service for personal gain.

A word of caution: Whenever the board decides to "go public," the chief executive should be kept fully informed. He or she should even have the opportunity to veto an idea. After all, the chief executive interacts constantly with the external constituency and should not be put in the position of having to explain a board initiative that he or she did not understand or support.

There are exceptions to the principles of board service that we are sharing in this book, but we believe the accountability of boards to their constituencies is good for the nonprofit sector. The excesses and bad practices of William Aramony, the ousted chief executive of United Way of America, the collapse of the fraudulent Foundation for New Era Philanthropy, and lapses at other nonprofit organizations have led the media, foundations, and individual donors to look for more evidence of strong boards. A commitment to open communication with constituencies is a step in the right direction.

SUGGESTED ACTION STEPS

1. Invite the board to reflect on the last time they linked directly with the organization's constituency.

2. List some examples of messages that would be more credible if they came from board members.

3. List the constituencies — current and prospective — your board should listen to as it plans for the future.

4. Consider developing a communications plan that includes the board.

---

1. John Carver, *Boards that Make a Difference*, 2nd ed. (San Francisco, CA: Jossey-Bass, 1997).

9

What is the board's responsibility to improve itself?

"Our chair thinks the board functions just fine, but I can tell you that many of us are very frustrated about our structure and our tendency to micromanage the staff."

This sentiment is common among board members. They seldom have the opportunity to give honest feedback about their perceptions of how the board is functioning. In fact, few boards are conscious of the need for some kind of formal evaluation. If even five percent of nonprofit boards now take the time to formally assess their own workings, we would be surprised.

Evaluation is a major function of any board. First, the board must assess whether the organization is carrying out its mission effectively. A good board also guarantees a fair, annual evaluation of the chief executive. To accomplish these various evaluation functions, many boards bring in outside experts to evaluate programs or financial matters such as the accounting system or the development strategy.

Sadly, most nonprofit boards give inadequate attention to these types of evaluations. A commercial enterprise finds out how well it is doing from the response of the marketplace. In the nonprofit sector, the governing board is a surrogate for the marketplace, assessing how well the organization's mission is being carried out. Evaluation is necessary for the board to fulfill this role.

One of the most neglected and sensitive of all board evaluation duties is the board's assessment of its own performance. Evaluation of the board is infrequently done for a number of reasons:

- Evaluation of peers is touchy business.

- No external entity requires it or even exerts pressure to do it.

- Few board members know how to coordinate an evaluation and fewer still volunteer to do it.

- The press of other urgent board business keeps the board from less pressing topics such as self-evaluation.

So why evaluate? The first challenge in carrying out an evaluation is to find at least a few board members willing to see the need for assessing the board's performance. Here are a few reasons why it is important:

- An organization, in the long run, is no better than its board. It is in everyone's interest to help the board function as effectively as it possibly can. Through these efforts, the organization will also improve.

- Board members become frustrated when they perceive that the board is dysfunctional in key areas. As a result, attendance at board meetings drops. It is surprising how few members resign. For some reason, many hang on with occasional participation, although they are tuned in with only half their brains.

- Staff morale suffers when the board doesn't seem interested in getting its act together. Staff trust and respect for the board wanes, and few chief executives on their own can fill that leadership vacuum.

- When a board can address its own needs honestly, it sends the right message to staff members that making mistakes and learning from them is natural and good.

- An effective board addresses issues, keeps the mission clear, uses funds wisely, and makes board meetings enjoyable. New member recruitment is easy.

APPROACHES TO EVALUATION

Boards unaccustomed to self-evaluation may wish to start with a fairly basic procedure. Several approaches follow, from simple to more complex. You may decide to create a hybrid process to fit your board's situation.

- *Regular board discussion.* Put on each board meeting agenda a 10- to 15-minute item called "Ideas for Improving Our Board." Since it is awkward for the chief executive to take independent initiative on evaluation, the board chair should be a champion of board improvement. The morale and loyalty of board members are stronger when the board is given the freedom to make suggestions. However, frank discussion also raises expectations that things will change. When a consensus is evident, the chair must be prepared to take action or refer ideas to a committee or task force for further consideration.

- *Board training as a stimulus.* Many boards lack consensus about board members' roles, individually or collectively. When that is the case, board members' ideas may lead the board to do the wrong things better. A session or two of board training — using a book, an outline, a veteran board member, or a consultant — can be an important help in setting standards against which the board can measure its own performance.

- *Board surveys.* Sometimes we begin consulting assignments with boards by creating with the chair and the chief executive a survey to be used with individual board members. A survey provides an agenda for discussing needed changes. It includes aspects of board life to be rated on a scale of one to five as well as a few open-ended questions. The board receives a summary of the responses, but no board member names are mentioned.

A simple survey should take a board member no longer than 10 to 15 minutes to complete. The answers reveal how much consensus there is about matters such as clarity of mission, board size, term of service, committee structure, the usefulness of board reports, quality of meetings, effectiveness of recruitment methods, and the quality of new-member orientation. Experience shows that the surveys should be returned to someone other than a current board or staff member. The response rate will be higher and the answers more candid. You might ask a respected former board member, a consultant, or someone else who is willing to tabulate and report the results.

An alternative to the single survey is several short surveys to cover various board functions. One survey could be presented and completed during each meeting, providing information and setting the stage for good discussion.

- *External audit*. Sometimes an expert on governance should be engaged to facilitate a more thorough evaluation. This person would be asked to undertake some or all of the following:
  1. Review the articles of incorporation and bylaws.
  2. Interview officers, other board members, the chief executive, and former board members.
  3. Observe board and committee meetings.
  4. Create and administer a mail or in-meeting survey.
  5. Facilitate a board discussion about key issues raised by the information gathered.

Employing an external consultant is usually less threatening than having your own leaders conduct a peer evaluation. By contracting with an expert who knows how other boards function, a board improves its chances of focusing on positive changes and increases its own level of interest and participation. A consultant is more objective than a member of the board and can offer alternatives for addressing problems. Usually, the consultant is in the best position to follow through with the board until it passes necessary bylaw amendments or policy resolutions. It is easy for boards to talk about improvements but to let months pass without taking action.

EVALUATION TOOLS

Some evaluation tools are designed for general use by several types of boards. One that meets the needs of most nonprofit organizations is published by BoardSource (formerly the National Center for Nonprofit Boards).[1] Some trade associations also have developed assessment instruments that include items appropriate to a particular sector.

TIMING FOR AN EVALUATION

Any time is better than no time for a board to evaluate its methods and procedures. Even an attempt that is not fully successful is usually better than no attempt at all. There are natural points in an organization's life cycle when formal evaluation is most useful. Two ideal occasions are the retirement of a long-standing chair or the departure of the chief executive. It is best *not* to initiate a formal evaluation when the organization is in a crisis, or to use it as a way to resolve personnel issues within the board. It is almost always wise to schedule the evaluation for a retreat or a special board meeting. The right setting can contribute a great deal to good dialogue.

A board evaluation might take longer than you think, so allow enough time to do a thorough job. It is impossible to complete an evaluation and deal constructively with all options for change in a single meeting. Allowing people to "sleep on ideas" is often useful. But we believe this kind of thorough evaluation should be focused in a six- to nine-month period.

Every board can improve in some areas. The regular rotation of board members requires that the board go through some evaluation process periodically as new members are identified. After you have done it once, a commitment to evaluate every three years is reasonable. Such a decision assumes you have set some standards against which you can measure progress.

CREATING A BOARD DEVELOPMENT COMMITTEE

The board chair must support the evaluation or at least be in sympathy with the process. However, the chair is usually too close to the issues to serve as facilitator. So is the chief executive, who is full of concerns and ideas but not in the best position to take an active role in the evaluation. We like the idea of creating a standing committee, sometimes called the governance or board development committee, to assume the traditional role of the nominating committee and to evaluate the board, orient new board members, review the bylaws periodically, and initiate board training when appropriate. This approach channels several related board functions to a single group. Often, the board vice-chair heads this committee.

PREPARING FOR THE COSTS

The costs of evaluation include personal risks and time as well as money. The participants risk being seen as judgmental. The chair risks the discovery that he or she is not meeting expectations. Evaluation takes time, especially since implementing the changes an evaluation mandates in itself may take time. The board must also decide on the percentage of the annual budget it is willing to commit to evaluation. Be prepared to budget for training publications or tapes, consultant fees and expenses, retreat expenses, and supplies and materials. Compared with other expenses, the financial investment in board evaluation is minimal when weighed against the potential benefits. If you believe that evaluation and professional development produce a first-class staff, why not apply the same principle to the board?

SUGGESTED ACTION STEPS

1. Take five minutes during a meeting to ask each board member to rank, on a scale of 1 to 10, how effective he or she thinks the governance process is.

2. Consider appointing a task force to do some research on board development. Prepare a survey of what board members need and want. Have the task force discuss these suggestions for how the board could be improved.

3. Commit to one three-hour training session with a proven board trainer. Then prepare an agenda for board development over a year or two.

---

1. National Center for Nonprofit Boards, *Self-Assessment for Nonprofit Governing Boards* (Washington, DC: National Center for Nonprofit Boards [now BoardSource], 1999).

Part II

Board Structure and Process

What is the best size for a board?

"We have 37 board members, but only about 20 are active."

To the question of size our answer is: "As few board members as are necessary to fulfill the board's role in the organization today." First, consider the legal requirement. Each state determines the minimum number of board members required to comply with its statutes on nonprofit corporations. We do not know of a state that requires more than three; some require only one. The national average is 19.[1] Given this baseline, your organization can consider several factors to determine board size.

Small boards can work for many organizations. Both of us have served on a board of three. We have also been chief executives for boards of 52 and 36. (That may explain our bias toward small boards.) If the criterion is getting the job done, a board can accomplish that and still have a variety of backgrounds and experiences with a well-selected board of seven or nine. An active, committed board of this size could eliminate the need for standing committees, although ad hoc committees might be used to help the board set policy in certain areas (for example, whether to purchase a building).

Small boards create genuine ownership among members. They are more aware of the big picture, know their participation is essential, build communication systems that work well, and achieve consensus more easily. A small board is more feasible if you also invite people from outside the board to serve on advisory groups, ad hoc task forces, or board committees.

Organizations that have many members or a diverse constituency may feel politically compelled to have a large board to properly represent all elements. One medical association, for example, represented many subspecialties. The group traditionally tried to have as board members doctors, paramedical personnel, scholars, and researchers. This national organization also wanted geographic representation, including someone from Canada, men and women, and at least one layperson representing the public. These needs appeared hard to achieve without assembling 30 or more board members. After a thorough review of these assumptions, however, the large board decided that a board of 12 would be more effective, efficient, and less costly.

Another example of a large board is a national organization with state affiliates. Many trade associations and professional societies find it difficult to exclude any state, so you start with 50 and debate from there. This approach seems reasonable, and it can work well.

Yet another philosophy fosters large boards: Board members are the major donors. We think there are dangers in using governing board membership as a primary recognition for significant contributions, but it happens. Many major donors lack the interest and motivation to deal with the broad range of board issues, but they have a hard time turning down the invitation. A real danger is when someone feels a financial donation should allow one board member to have more influence than others.

Large boards present other special challenges. Typically, they create active executive committees. Over time, this smaller group within the board takes on more and more of the policymaking. It is easier to get them together, to keep them informed, and to plan more efficient meetings. After a few years, tough issues in full board meetings are referred to the executive committee for action. Before long, the committee meets more often and the full board less often. A few board members not on the executive committee begin to skip meetings. They don't feel essential, so they decide (usually without telling anyone) to treat the board as a rubber stamp for the executive committee. They grow to feel more like advisors than members of the governing body. The chief executive has a difficult time personalizing relationships with all board members, so he or she focuses on the executive committee members. Other standing committees are created. Board members may feel somewhat informed about their committee areas of responsibility, but there is never enough time in full board meetings to feel informed about other areas.

Obviously, there is a price to pay for large size. Some large boards work quite well, however, and we don't want to criticize them. Tradition may be important. But ask yourself, "Could we function better with a smaller board?" If the answer is, "Yes, a smaller board would help us to pursue excellence in our governance system," we think it is wise to put the issue on the table.

If there are good reasons to justify a board of more than, say, 17, then it is important to structure the board so everyone feels meaningfully involved. Board communications become more important. Committees and good staff work to support them are critical. Building high expectations for attendance is key. A good, strong board chair to manage meetings is another critical element. We deal with some of these issues in upcoming chapters.

We need also to point out the weaknesses of trying to work with a board that is too small. Diversity of background, experience, and perspectives may be insufficient to address critical issues. There is the danger of getting in a rut, perhaps going too long with an old boys' (or girls') club that was brought on by the founder and resists the benefits of bringing new people into the leadership ranks. Then there is the real problem of asking a few to do too much, especially if a small board does not use outside task forces or others to help it in its governance task.

In the end, the answer to the question of board size is complicated and requires a careful analysis of the individual situation. We simply suggest that a historical decision on size not be accepted automatically as the best answer. As in other areas, an honest periodic evaluation may lead to better practices.

SUGGESTED ACTION STEPS

1. Take a confidential poll of your board members that asks what the ideal size of the board should be and whether the board should consider changing its size.

2. Take an informal survey of board size in similar organizations.

3. Ask your board to put in writing an argument for the best size at this time in the organization's life cycle.

---

1. National Center for Nonprofit Boards, *Nonprofit Governance Index* (Washington, DC: National Center for Nonprofit Boards [now BoardSource], 2000).

How should a board be structured?

*"We used to be totally dysfunctional. Now
we're accomplishing something."*

Many boards have enough capable people, a good mission statement, and other elements for success. But when an inefficient structure is perpetuated, board members become discouraged and their interest wanes. Board structure is one of the easiest things to create, maintain, and repair when necessary.

Let's look at one model that doesn't work. A board has 45 members with no term limits. The board chair is 82. He has served for 29 years because he was one of the founders and people hope he will leave much of his estate to the organization when he dies. Since he became chair, new committees have been created to address major issues. But they have no written job descriptions, and they tend to remain in existence far beyond their usefulness. Committee effectiveness depends on who is appointed committee chair. Some board members serve on as many as three committees. Need we go on?

The basic structure of board operations should be outlined in the bylaws. Bylaws should be changed whenever the majority of board members think there is a more efficient way to structure the organization. We have seen many options work well. There is no magic formula; the board leadership's willingness and ability to make the structure work is more important than following a textbook definition.

On the matter of basic structure, we offer these 10 suggestions:

1. Evaluate your structure every couple of years, and change it if 70 to 80 percent of board members favor a specific change. Tradition has its value, but not if it discourages board members from accomplishing their important roles.

2. Keep the board as small as possible to get the job done. Many large organizations work well with a board of 7 to 15 members. They may have no executive committee and just a few standing committees.

3. Evaluate the board chair as part of board evaluation. The nominating process must be open enough to find the best group process leader on the board to serve as its leader.

4. If a large board needs an executive committee, limit its authority in the bylaws to actions that are necessary between full board meetings. An executive committee that is allowed to do anything the full board can do gravitates to doing just that. Other board members begin to lose interest and feel unnecessary.[1]

5. In an organization that has paid staff, don't allow the volunteer board chair to act as the chief executive.

6. Clearly designate the chief executive as the sole agent of the board. All board business should flow through him or her, whether coming from board to staff or from staff to board.

7. Have as few standing committees as possible — for example, the audit committee and the governance or board development committee (nominations, education, evaluation). Do not frustrate the process by forming several committees on programs. One is enough. Insist that committees focus on activities that help the full

board do its work. Staff members do get advice from committees, but they should be allowed to seek advice from outside as well.

8. Use short-term, ad hoc task forces to address special needs of the board. Appoint the best people to these task forces, even if they are not board members. Be clear in charging the group to consider all the alternatives and make recommendations to the board.

9. Most boards of nonprofit organizations can benefit from the formation of an advisory group in addition to the board. The group need not meet for deliberation, but it provides visibility, credibility, and access to individual expertise. The chief executive is usually the best liaison to advisory group members. Often, they develop so much knowledge of the organization and interest in the board that they want to become board members.

10. Limit board membership to volunteers, with only one exception: the chief executive, and then only if the move appears to be wise. There are too many inherent conflicts of interest for staff to be voting on matters that affect them, such as acting as board employer of the chief executive while working as an employee. There is also a risk that volunteer board members will grow to depend on the knowledge of staff board members and never fully exercise their own governance roles. (For more about staff as board members, see Chapter 39.)

SUGGESTED ACTION STEPS

1. Ask your board to review our 10 suggestions. Which ones are you following? Which ones do not seem to fit your situation? Why not?

2. Contract with an outside facilitator, and ask each board member to write an unsigned memo to him or her outlining what they like and dislike about the current board structure. Ask for a summary report from the facilitator. Use the report as the starting point for a board discussion of how you could be more effective.

3. Appoint a task force to review the structure of five organizations similar to yours and report ideas back to the board.

---

1. Robert C. Andringa, *The Executive Committee: Making It Work for Your Organization* (Washington, DC: National Center for Nonprofit Boards [now BoardSource], 1994).

Does a board need an executive committee?

"I think we can function just fine
without an executive committee."

Tradition is no reason for deciding whether to have an executive committee. Whether your board has always — or never — had one, you need a rationale that is sensible. Two key principles define the role of an executive committee:

- It should not be a complete surrogate for the board itself.
- Its decisions should be affirmed by the full board.

Unlike other standing committees, the executive committee is established to speak *to* the board as well as *for* the board. It speaks to the board whenever the board gives this committee responsibility over an aspect of governance — reviewing the bylaws, re-examining the mission statement, or evaluating the organization's goals. The committee would meet to deliberate on these issues and recommend changes to the board. The executive committee speaks for the board when the board gives the committee authority to act on its behalf. This second role is the most common reason for establishing an executive committee.

There are significant benefits to providing this backup system. For international, national, or regional boards that meet only a few times a year, an executive committee is a mechanism for convening a smaller number of people to make timely board decisions. For large boards, the executive committee is a more workable group for dealing with issues other boards might handle in full session. For organizations that are in the midst of major restructuring, growth, or a merger and require frequent board decisions, an executive committee that can meet on short notice — by telephone conference call or in person — makes good sense.

Over time and for a variety of reasons, an executive committee can inadvertently take on responsibilities and decisions that belong to the full board, and it is wise to be alert to this risk. An executive committee that meets monthly when the board meets only three times a year will move matters along more quickly. Or a board chair and chief executive may decide that full board meetings are too divisive, get bogged down in details, never finish the agenda, or suffer from lack of quorums. Instead of trying to fix the board problems, they divert decisions to the executive committee and marginalize the authority and commitment of many board members. Board members' commitment may also suffer if they begin to feel that they are asked to rubber stamp the executive committee's decisions.

How can you bring balance to this frequent tension in governance? If your board has not reached clear consensus on whether to have an executive committee, you can take an intermediate approach that provides a good insurance policy. Amend the bylaws to specify that the board *may* establish an executive committee to act on behalf of the board, when necessary, between regular board meetings.

When authorizing an executive committee, put reasonable limits on its authority. For example: "The executive committee may not amend the bylaws, hire or terminate the chief executive, elect or terminate board members, purchase or sell property, or dissolve the organization. Notices and minutes of executive committee meetings must be provided to all board members. All actions of the executive committee are subject to later review by the board."

The board chair almost always chairs the executive committee, and the chief executive usually staffs it. If the chief executive is an *ex officio* member of the board, then he or she should have the same status on the executive committee. Minutes of other standing committees may not be necessary because board action is taken and recorded at the full board level, but executive committee minutes should be prepared and sent within a week or two to all board members. At its next meeting the full board should confirm the committee's decisions to eliminate any doubt in the official record and to be sure the entire board is aware of those board actions.

SUGGESTED ACTION STEPS

1. In light of where the board and the organization are today, have the board ask: Do we need an executive committee? If so, how should its authority be limited, and how often should it meet?

2. Evaluate the minutes of the last four or five board meetings to see which low-priority issues could have been given to an executive committee so the board itself could have focused on the major strategic issues.

⑬

What is the role of
the board chair?

"I see my role of chair as the manager of the board."

Throughout this book we will remind you that if roles are clearly understood, the partnership between the board chair and the chief executive will help the organization flourish. If these two organizational leaders have a private compact to do whatever is necessary to make each other successful, the success of the board and the organization will follow.

What can stand in the way of a board chair's effectiveness? First, some board members treat their chair as if he or she is the chief executive. They ask questions and set expectations that should be focused on the staff leader of the organization. When the board chair carries the title of president, the situation can be confusing and the problem compounded.

Some organizations get started without full time paid staff. In those cases, the board chair often plays the dual role of running board meetings and serving as the senior implementor of policy. Habits develop. When a paid chief executive is hired, roles must be clearly delineated or people will continue to look to the board chair for day-to-day leadership. The chief executive is treated like a chief operating officer or manager rather than like a chief executive. Even the bylaws may not get changed, so the picture of who plays what role is cloudy.

Another problem arises when a chief executive, particularly one who was a founder of the organization, views the board chair as a competitor or a threat. The executive never brings in the chair between meetings for consultation on agendas, board development, committee structure, or other matters. The goal is to keep the chair in the dark except when he or she is presiding over formal business meetings.

Unfortunately, some of these strong founder-chief executives write the script (often in the bylaws) that they will function as *both* chief executive and board chair. Why share the power? We have seen only a few situations in which this structure works. Here are the main reasons we think it is a poor model:

- Two are better than one in understanding, relating to, encouraging, and nurturing a board.

- Accountability is so important in maintaining the credibility of a nonprofit organization that a chief executive needs to prevent the obvious and inevitable conflicts of interest that come from chairing the board as well as supervising the staff.

- The chief executive needs someone (the board chair) who can translate board feelings and actions that would not otherwise be communicated.

- Boards need to feel important, needed, and strategically significant to organizational success. This happens more readily when one of their own is viewed in a leadership role.

In a startup organization, the dual-role model may be the only option. But in an organization with even one professional staff member, we suggest a time limit of one or two years before separating the roles and writing job descriptions.

Assuming that the organization has a clearly identified chief executive and a volunteer board chair, here are the chair's basic responsibilities.

1. Preside at board meetings.

This is a skill. Some are elected chair because of their tenure on the board, their close relationship with the chief executive, their major donations (or hoped-for major donations), their personal popularity, pure politics, or the fact that they were there first and the bylaws and organizational culture simply leave the same chair in place until he or she dies.

We urge that the ability to manage group process be a primary consideration in officer elections. If you have a plausible argument for keeping a good board chair with poor meeting skills, then we suggest appointing a vice-chair who is skilled at presiding to fulfill this task. Keep the chair for other important functions but ask him or her to agree that turning the gavel over to the vice-chair after brief opening remarks at business meetings is best for the organization.

2. Coauthor board agendas.

The organization's leadership sets the agenda for board meetings. The board chair and chief executive should discuss well in advance of a meeting what should be on the agenda, how much time to give key items, whether guests should be invited to make presentations, how long staff reports should take (most can be sent out in advance), and whether to have an executive session without staff present.

3. Appoint and assist committees.

Whether the bylaws give appointment authority to the full board or to the chair, the board chair should have considerable influence in committee assignments. This responsibility requires knowing the interests and availability of all board members. It also calls for fairness and balance in matching personalities to group tasks. Consultation is always required, but the board chair is the one who understands the strengths and weaknesses of the volunteers on the board and of the chief executive. He or she is most aware of the broad picture. This appointment authority is a strategic power to have and to handle with care.

Most bylaws make the board chair an *ex officio* member of all committees, but few board chairs have the time to attend many meetings. This is understandable, but we urge board chairs to invest some orientation time up front with at least the committee chair, if not with each committee. Everyone benefits from knowing the board chair's expectations, the time frame for decisions, and the committee's authority to call on staff for help. After all, if a chair has good committees working, the headaches of board leadership are reduced.

One special responsibility of the board chair is appointing and issuing the charge to a search committee for a new chief executive. Some chairs finish their tenure without having to face this difficult task, but when the organization needs to recruit and hire a new chief executive, the board chair usually plays the key role. No top candidate should say yes to an offer without interacting with the board chair and feeling good about the role he or she plays in the organization. (We address the task of recruiting a new chief executive in Chapter 44.)

4. Manage group development.

Someone must be thinking constantly about making the board work effectively and efficiently. Some decisions — such as board size, term of service, and committee structure — are group decisions codified in the bylaws or standing policies. But the board chair is often the one to recommend changes in board policy. Many other group process decisions are left to the chair's discretion. When should special meetings be called? Should a certain issue be referred to a committee or discussed immediately by the full board? How should we evaluate ourselves? How should we evaluate the chief executive? Should inactive board members be terminated?

5. Maintain organizational integrity.

No other leader has more legal and moral authority to maintain organizational integrity than the board chair. An arm's-length relationship to daily operations is necessary in order to fulfill this role objectively. Most organizations can survive temporary crises; few can survive the loss of public trust. The board chair's internal watch is critical because few volunteer board members take the time, or exercise the courage, to tackle the real issues. In our opinion, every board member must help fulfill this role. What's more, the board chair must set the tone for this important task.

Some point out that the chief executive has this responsibility, too. In some areas, however, the chief executive is simply too close to the action to view certain issues as the organization's moral owners would see them. Obvious examples include executive compensation, treatment of honoraria and book royalties, definition of allowable expenses, truthfulness in fund-raising appeals, and treatment of women and ethnic minorities — the list is long, and the board chair must pay attention.

6. Support the chief executive.

In our experience, few chief executives have a good read on their board. They think they do, but most board members are reluctant to be totally frank with their chief executive, whom they normally love but also wish would change this or that. The board chair needs to keep an ear to the ground, sound out individual board members, and then gently encourage the chief executive in the direction of positive board relationships. Chief executives need encouragement as well as feedback on their behavior. They usually like affirmation from the board chair. A kind note, a quick call to check on the family, an offer to go have fun together — these build the foundation of a relationship that will withstand inevitable times of tension.

7. Link with the major moral owners.

One of the tasks of a board is to stay in touch with the organization's major constituencies. While staff do this constantly, there are times when the board chair is the most appropriate person to represent the organization at a key meeting, be on a radio talk show, write a magazine column, hold a press conference, preside at a focus group, make a presentation at a community forum, or thank major donors. It is quite obvious when the board chair is in a better position than the chief executive to play this visible outside role. Often they get the best results from doing something together.

The board chair's role is far from honorary. We believe the board chair is critical to the well-being of the organization. If this role is not filled well, board members become discouraged, the chief executive gets frustrated, staff lose confidence in their board leaders, and things get overlooked. Furthermore, the organization could be vulnerable to an IRS audit or other legal problems, and the mission is diluted or put in jeopardy.

The board chair's task is so critical that some feel he or she should be paid. At the least, offer frequent words of appreciation. Your chair deserves it!

SUGGESTED ACTION STEPS

1. Schedule a lunch between the board chair and chief executive to discuss this chapter and draft a mutually agreeable role description for the chair. Present to the board any necessary changes in the bylaws or standing policies so everyone is making the same assumptions and holding the chair to the same expectations.

2. After everyone is clear about the board chair's role, allow the chair to benefit from a board evaluation of how well he or she is fulfilling it.

3. Schedule an informal meeting exclusively for five or six board chairs of nonprofit organizations of similar size in the community. Let them talk shop as one way of developing their own knowledge and skills.

14

How should a board select its officers?

"For years we've simply re-elected the old officers by acclamation."

Board officers are the leaders of the board. They provide conceptual leadership and model the board's working culture — the tone and approach for its interactions. From a practical standpoint, officers coordinate board activities and are responsible for special assignments. Most boards have a chair, vice-chair, and treasurer. Some boards still elect a secretary; however, in current practice, staff members often carry out the duties of secretary and, to some extent, treasurer.

Most organizations elect volunteers to the traditional four posts and then elect an assistant secretary to actually keep the minutes, send out information, and maintain the official records. The assistant treasurer is usually the organization's chief financial staff member, who actually maintains and reports on finances.

These principles can ensure the election of capable officers:

- Elect people whose strengths fit the task.

- Elect each officer annually, after the nominating committee has evaluated current officers.

- Do not establish strict term limits for officers as long as each officer receives a positive evaluation and the person is willing to continue. A reasonable compromise is a limit of four or five one-year terms so that others have a chance to serve in these leadership positions.

For most boards, the job of chair requires the greatest time commitment. The chair manages the board and serves as the primary liaison between the board and the chief executive. The other officers can play significant roles if their jobs are well defined. For example, a vice-chair might head the board development committee or facilitate the chief executive's annual performance review. The secretary may oversee the documentation of a records management system for the board. The treasurer might help the board define what format is best for board financial reports. If there is an executive committee, the officers are almost always on that committee, contributing their leadership skills as a group. Some boards combine the positions of secretary and treasurer when staff essentially fulfill both roles. Some boards elect the chief financial officer as board treasurer, but not as a voting board member.

How board officers are elected requires careful consideration. Let's start by eliminating poor rationales, such as who has served the longest, who has the most free time, who lives closest to the office, who is the biggest donor, or who the chief executive wants. The skills, experience, and temperament of a person are far more important qualifications.

THREE COMMON WAYS TO ELECT OFFICERS

There are three common ways to elect officers. The board should discuss these options and decide what is best for the organization given its culture and personality.

1. Adoption of an uncontested slate

The first — and preferred — method is by adopting an uncontested slate. The nominating — or governance — committee looks at all the possibilities, talks informally with board members and potential candidates, and presents a slate of officers to the full board. If the process has been open and careful, the slate is adopted with no nominations from the floor. When the committee presents two or more candidates for each position, each board member has a choice to make. But this approach tends to create "losers" and affect board morale. The preferred method is to have a strong committee communicating between board members and candidates that results in a single candidate who is backed by everyone.

2. Selection by a parent organization or outside appointing authority

The second approach is the selection of officers by a parent organization or an outside appointing authority. In this case, the same entity probably appoints or elects all board members. This method is less effective because the appointing authorities may not actually see how these officers perform. Internal politics may also unduly influence the selection.

3. Open election

The third option is an open election. For each officer position, an envelope is passed around the table. Each board member writes a name on an index card and inserts it into the envelope. Someone tallies and announces the vote. If no one receives a majority, the envelope is passed around again, until one person receives a majority of the board's votes. The process is repeated until all officers are elected. One can argue that this process yields officers who have the trust of every board member. It also gives the elected officer a sense of confidence and accountability to do the job well.

There is value in the third approach, especially if the board has felt that a group of insiders controls elections. But there are a few limitations. A candidate may stay in the race simply because he or she feels flattered to have been considered. The process also makes it difficult for the chief executive to express concerns about the candidates. And it may not produce officers who are well matched to their jobs. In spite of these drawbacks, an open election does prevent board members from feeling left out of the process.

Some boards promote the vice-chair to chair when the chair's term ends. This system ensures that incoming chairs are more experienced in board leadership, but it is not without problems. Life changes for people, and it may be difficult for a vice-chair to project that far ahead. It is better to wait until the time comes and nominate the candidate who is best prepared to serve as chair. Besides, if a chair is performing with excellence, why make a change?

SUGGESTED ACTION STEPS

1. Ask the board development committee or a small group of experienced board members to think about the way officers are elected and evaluated and recommend changes.

2. Consider electing an assistant secretary and assistant treasurer from the staff to do the work the bylaws may prescribe for the secretary and treasurer. Or think about moving the secretary's and treasurer's jobs from volunteers to staff.

15

How can we keep track of evolving board policies?

"If the truth were known, our board members have no idea what policies earlier boards put on the books."

Can you remember the policies your board put into the minutes five years ago? One year ago? Even during the last meeting? Most board members cannot, and somehow they believe the chief executive or the board secretary keeps track of such things for them.

There are some persuasive reasons for keeping board policies organized and accessible:

- The board is liable for its own policies in a court of law.

- Staff members need to be clear on exactly what they are supposed to implement.

- Board members should not have to reinvent similar policies over and over again.

The solution is deceptively simple: Have one document in which all the ongoing policies that the board adopts are maintained. This board policy manual is a useful tool that helps the board speak with one voice on critical matters, guiding it and the staff until the board chooses to make changes. Writing good, comprehensive policies is hard work. It is not done overnight, but it is worth the effort. And the document never needs to exceed 20 pages.

We like the policy governance model found in John Carver's book *Boards that Make a Difference.*[1] Carver develops the theory and methodology of writing standing policies as part of his overall paradigm. In this chapter, we address specifically how board members can remember policies agreed upon in the past.

Except for routine motions listed in the organization's minutes, these written standing policies may be organized in a board policy manual that contains *all* the standing policies of the organization as they have been added to or modified over time. Here are the steps to developing a standing policies manual.

1. Get the board to understand and agree.

Most boards will acknowledge readily the problem of lost policies. Ultimately they must vote on the newly created standing policies, so they need to give their permission to start the task. Getting board approval of all initial standing policies could take a year or two.

Each board member needs to understand the hierarchy of legal authority within which the standing policies fit. Here it is:

a. Federal and state laws, including Internal Revenue Service regulations and legally binding contracts;

b. Articles of incorporation for the organization;

c. Bylaws of the organization;

d. Standing policies of the organization;

e. Other one-time, short-term policies found in the board minutes; and

f. Administrative decisions made by staff; personnel policies and procedures.

No action at any one level within this hierarchy may violate the rules set in the level above it. When a board changes the articles of incorporation (for example, the name or purpose of an organization), it must submit the changes to the appropriate state authorities, but boards rarely do this. The board can—and should—change its bylaws whenever they can be improved. Most boards do so every few years.

The board can add to, amend, or eliminate specific standing policies whenever it finds a better way to state that policy. Once the standing policies manual is under way, the board likely will change it at some level during every meeting. In fact, since setting policy is the main role of the board, the manual should be the major reference tool at board meetings.

Whenever an issue surfaces, the first question to ask is, "What do our standing policies say?" If there is nothing in print to guide the organization, the next question is, "What policy should we adopt to cover this and similar situations in the future?"

Each chapter of the policies manual is based on the explicit understanding that someone has authority to make decisions within the context of the policies. Usually this person is the chief executive. In chapters relating to how the board functions, the board chair has the authority. In essence, board members understand that at some point these policies could become so detailed that the board moves beyond policy making and begins to invade staff administrative prerogatives. The board's consensus on when to stop writing more detailed policies is important. Board members should keep their policies at the broad governance level.

2. Establish major policy areas.

In Carver's book the four major areas relate to:

- Ends policies (such as mission and goals);

- Limitations on the means (to guide staff in implementing the ends policies);

- Board-staff relations (to spell out personnel, reporting, and other policies); and

- Board structure policies (to amplify the bylaws in spelling out how the board manages its own affairs).

Some nonprofits organize the board standing policies manual into more specific sections. Typical choices might be: mission, board structure and process, finances, program, fund-raising, board-staff relations, and the ever-necessary "miscellaneous." If you think through your own best table of contents, the writing task will be easier. But you can always rearrange the section headings once you are into the project.

3. Assign the drafting team.

Usually the chief executive is in the best position to draft policies for board review because he or she is thinking about the organization every day and is most aware of what's needed. However, since setting board policy is the board's responsibility, a board-staff team of two also can be effective. The drafters' initial job is to reflect as accurately and succinctly as possible the current policies of the organization. They should develop straightforward statements communicating current policy, whether found in the oral tradition or in the organization's documents (such as minutes, publications, or personnel manuals).

4. Write a first draft.

If you are fortunate enough to have minutes with clear, distinct policy resolutions, it may be possible to copy them from old minutes into the policy manual's appropriate sections. This procedure is usually difficult because many older policies are written on specific issues. They may lack the quality and clarity needed to guide decisions on similar issues. Therefore, the easiest approach is to assemble the old policy statements as reference material (although they continue to be legally binding until superseded). They guide the drafting team in restating similar policies for the draft policies manual.

Clear, succinct statements are critical, so don't put a lot of legalese in these policies. John Carver has a good perspective on the process. Start with broad statements and become increasingly specific until the board has said enough. From there, the board delegates to the chief executive (or the board chair, depending on the policy) decisions consistent with the policies. See Figure 5 for suggestions on what to include in a board standing policies manual.

5. Ask legal counsel to review the drafts.

Once the drafting begins, bring the organization's legal counsel into the picture to review the document. The attorney should not write policies, but he or she will certainly have many helpful suggestions including how new policies should be adopted in a way that old, related policies can then be discontinued.

6. Present drafts to the board for approval.

Once the drafting team has sections ready for board approval, we suggest a first reading at a board meeting to give the writers informal feedback. After the team incorporates those suggestions, send the next draft to board members well in advance of the next board meeting, when the board can formally adopt its first standing policies manual. You may decide to adopt one chapter or major section at a time. At succeeding meetings, new sections are presented within the framework of the original table of contents and earlier adopted policies. Eventually, by resolution drafted by legal counsel, terminate all previous policies that may conflict with these new ones.

7. Continue to review and revise board policies.

After the major work is done, do not forget about standing policies. Use the policies manual as a resource. Continue to review policies for effectiveness. At some point, few policy changes will be required. Creating a policies manual is a proactive step that promotes efficient governance and management. Staff are free to initiate actions within the context of policies instead of taking every decision to the board for approval. When you reach this point, your board is well on its way to governing effectively.

Figure 5

SUGGESTED OUTLINE FOR A BOARD STANDING POLICIES MANUAL

I.   Mission, Values, Strategies, and Major Goals

1.1   Vision

1.2   Mission

1.3   Values to guide us

1.4   Major board goals to guide the staff strategic plan

2   Board Structure and Process

2.1   Philosophy of governance

2.2   Criteria for board membership

2.3   Board meetings

2.4   Committees and their job descriptions

2.5   Board expenses

3.   Board-Staff Relations

3.1   Board guidance on hiring, compensation, and treatment of staff

3.2   Evaluation of the chief executive

3.3   Reports from staff to board

Board Parameters on Staff Actions *(often a chapter for each committee to oversee)*

4.   Financial Parameters

4.1   Budget guidelines

4.2   Debt

4.3   Risk management

4.4   Investment policies

4.5   Audit

5.   Program Parameters

5.1   Limitations on "means" to achieve the board's "ends" policies

5.2   Other boundaries regarding major programs—*what the board wants or does not want*

6.   Membership Parameters *(if applicable)*

7.   Fund-Raising Parameters *(similar to Chapter 5 on program parameters)*

8.   Miscellaneous Policies

SUGGESTED ACTION STEPS

1. Ask your board what its policy is in five or six areas and when it was enacted. Illustrate the problem of forgotten policies by drawing from old minutes.

2. Have board officers read John Carver's *Boards that Make a Difference* for advice on policy governance and policies manuals.

3. Bring to a board meeting a one-page draft relating to one aspect of the organization. Ask whether it reflects current practice. Does the board see the value of putting in writing what may be only assumed by some?

---

1. John Carver, *Boards that Make a Difference*, 2nd ed. (San Francisco, CA: Jossey-Bass, 1997).

⑯

How should board minutes be written, approved, and kept?

"Our minutes read like a novel — who said what on everything!"

Minutes from a board meeting are the permanent record that provides information about when the meeting occurred and what action was taken. Some organizations follow strict formats, while others take a more informal approach. Regardless of how you present the minutes of your board meeting, consider carefully what you want to include in this document. Just about the only absolute rule is that minutes are legally required of a corporation. Beyond that, consider these points:

I. Who should take minutes?

In rare instances, the elected board secretary actually takes minutes. More often, a staff member is assigned to the task. That person takes detailed notes and sometimes tapes the meeting as a backup (though taping is thought by some to hinder an open discussion and may present legal concerns as well).

2. How much detail should be written down?

There is a difference between the final minutes and the notes or tape from the meeting, which could be helpful afterward to the chair and chief executive as well as to the person writing the formal minutes. Some attorneys advise writing detailed minutes because they could help you should you ever go to court. But others maintain that minutes should be brief, recording only formal actions, in case they become part of the discovery process in a lawsuit. Every organization should consult its legal counsel on this matter. From the perspective of board members and chief executives, effective minutes allow readers to determine easily what decisions were made but not necessarily to understand all the deliberations. Short minutes — two pages on a four-hour board meeting — are adequate.

3. What is the best format?

Each board should determine its own style. A predetermined format is practical because it is easier to write and read. A uniform heading is useful when reviewing several sets of minutes. Minutes should begin with the date, place, starting time, board members present, and board members absent. Each page should have a footer indicating the organization name, date, and page number. The narrative should summarize routine opening business and then introduce each item of board business followed by the board decision. The minutes can use shorthand similar to this: "MSC: Bob Jones be elected chair for two years from this annual meeting" (MSC means moved, seconded, and carried). It is not necessary to record who made or seconded a motion.

4. How are minutes approved?

When a staff member drafts the minutes, it may be wise to circulate them for content edits to other staff who attended the meeting, then send them in draft form to the elected board secretary. The minutes might be signed, "Written by Steve Stickler and approved by Sam Secretary." With that step accomplished, they should be mailed to the entire board within two weeks of the meeting. They usually appear again in the advance materials for the next board meeting, at which time they are formally approved, with any amendments, for safekeeping.

5. Where should minutes be kept?

The assistant board secretary or a staff member should store board minutes in files or notebooks in a secure area. The electronic files should also be retained, with a backup set stored off site. Some organizations maintain a board reference book that includes minutes of the last three or four meetings. This portable board library, kept up to date by a staff member, is available at all board meetings. It should include other useful reference documents, such as the bylaws, a list of board members, committee assignments, the last budget and audit, and a list of staff and programs.

6. What about committee minutes?

Executive committee minutes should be kept in a similar fashion and distributed to all board members, who should affirm the committee's decisions at their next meeting. Whether other committees should keep minutes is a matter of choice. Since most committees are only shaping recommendations to the board, minutes are not legally necessary. They are useful for absent committee members, the board chair, or even all board members — but keep them short.

7. What if the board has a standing policies manual?

In this case, board minutes can be even shorter. Policy changes can be noted in the minutes with a simple statement like this: "During the meeting, the board reviewed committee recommendations for changing the standing policies and adopted those listed here, now reflected in the May 15, 2001, version: 1.4, 1.7. 2.6.2, 3.5, 4.2.3, and 7.2." Send the minutes with the revised policies manual to board members (remember that it is only 15 to 20 pages long). Of course, electronic files of each version of the policies manual are retained for reference. But that need is highly unlikely because it is the current policies that are important.

8. Should minutes be available on the Web?

Some board members may want electronic access to the minutes and policies manual by e-mail or the organization's Web site. You might want to make this information available only with a password. But never deny board members their own hard copies.

Some boards add bells and whistles — such as topical headings or color-coding — to their meeting minutes. But most board members are happy with crisp, clear, accurate minutes that reflect just the facts, and they are more than willing to leave to good memories all the dialogue that went into the decisions.

SUGGESTED ACTION STEPS

1. Take a straw vote on whether your board wants shorter or more detailed minutes.

2. Be sure the location of the minutes is known. If the task has been neglected, set up a new system in which several people know where to find them if needed.

3. If the elected board secretary has been taking minutes, consider delegating the job to a staff member.

17

How can committees be most effective?

"We have too many committees that aren't doing anything."

Committees are simply one way a governing board organizes itself to be more efficient and effective. Some boards have no committees. Most find it helpful to have a few committees and task forces.

According to research by Chait, Holland, and Taylor, the most effective boards organize themselves around issues that matter. Substance dictates board structure.[1]

One board was in as bad a shape as you can imagine. The bylaws provided for six standing committees and allowed for others at the board's discretion. Various committees were appointed over time, some called ad hoc, some special, and a few standing. The board elected the executive committee and the finance committee. The board chair appointed the other committees, but the current chair didn't think some were necessary so she did not appoint members to them. A few of the "old" committees continued to meet from time to time, a practice the chair evidently felt was not important enough to stop.

You don't need to be in chaos over committees. We suggest your board think through these questions:

- Do we want committees, or can the full board deal with all business itself?

- If we want standing committees, which do we need now? (Needs change over the years.)

- Should we amend our bylaws to reflect our decisions about committees? We suggest that the details of committees be documented in standing policies. The bylaws could simply authorize the board to "create such standing or other committees or task forces as the board may determine from time to time and describe in its standing policies."

- When we decide which committees we want, how should we describe their functions, size, membership, staffing, and appointment process? (These details can be contained in a few paragraphs of the standing policies.)

WHICH COMMITTEES?

The typical lineup is executive committee, finance committee (often serving as the audit committee as well, though not recommended), program committee (sometimes broken into two or three program-related committees), board development or governance committee (a new idea for many boards), and development or advancement committee (focused on fund-raising).

Although many organizations still maintain these traditional committees, it's important for the board to keep in mind the work that needs to be done and allocate board resources accordingly. We suggest keeping the number manageable and appropriate to the organization's needs.

WHO CAN SERVE?

The bylaws should allow a board to appoint some committee members from outside the board. This practice enables you to bring on expertise that the board itself may not have — an investment advisor for the finance committee, for example. You will be able to groom future board members and involve people who are willing to volunteer on a focused issue but are not yet ready to commit to the full role of a board member. Because most board members are busy people, we also feel it is best to ask each to serve on only one standing committee. They might also be appointed to an ad hoc task force (typically a smaller group with a focused assignment that is completed within a set time and then disbanded).

WHO SHOULD CHAIR COMMITTEES?

You want a good manager of people and process, someone who feels confident in guiding committee members to accomplish the task in a timely fashion. The job requires extra homework, time in communication with staff, a willingness to resolve conflicts among members, and a commitment to keep the board chair informed at all times. It is not an honorary role.

WHO APPOINTS OR ELECTS MEMBERS?

Someone has to match individual board members to the committees' needs. Putting together the right mix of people is also important. If the board has a board development committee (see Chapter 9), this committee might perform the task. Often, the board chair and the chief executive are best equipped to map out committee assignments. A good policy to include in bylaws might then read, "The chair shall appoint committee members and chairs, subject to the approval of the full board."

WHAT IS THE COMMITTEE'S ROLE?

Committee roles can vary, so of greatest importance is to agree upon the committee's role and charge at the outset. If you follow our policy model, the basic role of standing committees is to draft changes to standing policies and present them to the board for adoption. If a committee does this well, it might also have time to serve as a sounding board, giving advice to the senior staff member responsible for managing the area of the committee's responsibility. Please note: A committee speaks *to* the board, not *for* the board. Committees cannot think and act as "small boards." They do not set board policy. And we think senior managers ought to be free to get advice from many sources, not just from board committees. Remember, advice to staff usually comes when board members are wearing their volunteer hats (see Chapter 2), and this applies to advice from committees, for the most part.

WHO STAFFS THE COMMITTEE?

Some organizations have few staff members, requiring the chief executive to staff almost every committee. A committee member might be asked to take minutes of meetings. Larger organizations typically have an executive whose role fits the committee's role and is asked by the chief executive to staff the committee. The board might set a policy that the chief executive will assign a staff member to work with each committee chair in preparing agenda material, maintaining good communications, and preparing minutes. It is important for the staff liaison to remember that he or she still reports to the chief executive and only helps the committee fulfill its assignment. We have seen situations in which a vice-president who may not always agree with the chief executive begins to use the line, "But my committee told me to stop that project." This is the time to remind people that the board speaks with one voice, usually leaving policy implementation to the chief executive, who then delegates to other staff.

We discuss committee meetings in Part IV.

THE EXECUTIVE COMMITTEE

There is no other committee with more potential to help — or to hinder — good governance. Usually when a board gets larger than 15 members, someone will suggest creating an executive committee. The most common rationale is to have a small group that can meet more easily than the full board to approve things more quickly. Clearly, when a board gets larger than 30 or so, especially if board members are scattered across the country or the world, an executive committee is helpful. Some executive committees assume a primary role in discussing critical issues before recommending a course of action to the full board. In this role, they function much like a program or finance committee.

The danger of executive committees, as we mention in other chapters, is that the full board may relax its sense of commitment and accountability, knowing that the executive committee can act on its behalf. Board members who are not on an active executive committee can develop a we-they attitude that "insiders" are making all the key decisions. Attendance at full board meetings can drop. The unity of the board can be damaged. Some board members, not wanting to deal with difficult or unpopular issues, are prone to say, "I move we refer this to the executive committee for action." That attitude undermines the very reason a diverse group of people were elected to the board.

A board should write into its bylaws some parameters on the authority of the executive committee.[2] For example, we don't believe executive committees should be able to change the bylaws, elect officers, or hire or fire the chief executive. The right job description for this powerful committee can, however, complement the work and realities of a fully involved board. See Chapter 12 for more on executive committees.

Committees are a structural tool, available to but not required of any board. They should not become mini-boards with their own authority, nor should they be groups that advise staff. But by their specialized focus they can be of immense help in developing wise recommendations for board policy. And they usually add to a board member's enjoyment of board service.

SUGGESTED ACTION STEPS

1. Clarify in your policies or minutes why you have committees and which should be ongoing standing committees. (You may be surprised that the board no longer feels some are necessary.)

2. If you have an executive committee, write a job description that makes clear its relationship to the full board.

3. Consider how new temporary (some call them special) committees or task forces might be used to get attention focused on a hot topic that the current structure has difficulty dealing with.

---

1. Taylor et al, "The New Work of the Board," in *Harvard Business Review,* September/October 1996 (Boulder, CO: Harvard Business Review, 1996).

2. Andringa, *The Executive Committee: Making It Work for Your Organization.*

18

What if a board member opposes a board decision?

"George just won't give up on his insistence that we are wrong."

If a board of 17 always agrees on everything, why not just have a board of three? Divergent opinions on a board are good — but ultimately boards must speak with one voice.

Here are some principles to guide board discussion:

- Once elected, every board member should think and act for the good of the whole; even if some are selected from a particular group or region, their ultimate loyalty must be to the organization as a whole.

- Encourage different points of view at the time an issue is being discussed.

- When everyone feels that the discussion process has been fair and complete, call for a vote.

- The majority determines the board's decision, and everyone is obligated to support the decision.

The board should review these principles from time to time because they are critical to good governance. When a board member continually violates them, the chair should invite him or her to breakfast to remind the board member of the duty of loyalty which obligates board members to act in the best interest of the organization as a whole.

Disagreements within the boardroom are proper and expected, as long as everyone models for one another how to disagree agreeably. Board members need to separate the policy difference from the person. How a board member expresses disagreement is often more important than the difference of opinion itself. But once everyone has had a fair chance to debate the issue, the board should act, and the minority should stop airing his or her objections.

A more difficult and onerous problem is the board member who takes the disagreement public. Once the board has acted, it is important that every board member fairly represent the will of the board to whomever is in the conversation. Continuing to argue one's minority view outside the board meeting with staff, donors, or others is out of bounds. Sometimes board members simply need a reminder about this very human instinct. If they disagree and continue taking the fight to the streets, they should be asked to resign. And the board should be willing to apply the ultimate sanction — termination of membership — if a recalcitrant board member continues this poor behavior.

Here are some reasons why board members may disagree:

- *Lack of clarity.* The policy was never expressed very clearly and is subject to different interpretations. The solution is to redraft the resolution or policy so any reasonable person will interpret it correctly.

- *Lack of policy guidance.* There was never a board decision on some important matter, and one persistent board member keeps insisting that there should be a board policy. Maybe the chair or chief executive has resisted board action. Usually, open discussion will resolve this problem. Either the matter is delegated to the staff, or the board acts. Restricting any member from putting a strongly held concern on the table is risky.

- *Reluctance to challenge.* The staff is not adhering to a board policy, and, for whatever reasons, the board is not willing to hold the chief executive accountable. This situation often raises the hackles of at least one board member who opposes silence on the matter. The board should listen to any modification in the policy the chief executive recommends and then make a clear decision, expecting the chief executive to honor the board's action.

- *Lack of monitoring data.* The board never defined how to monitor the effectiveness of its policy. So some board members think the policy is wrong; others believe it is correct. The solution is to gather data to assure the board that it has a good policy or gain the information needed to change it.

- *Pressure from a donor board member.* A major donor insists on having his or her way and threatens to stop giving. This is an opportunity for good board chairs to earn their keep by asking the donor–board member to breakfast. Sometimes the answer is clear, as when a donor's request is in conflict with the organization's mission. In situations where the answer is less clear, the board chair must explain the board's rationale for rejecting a donor's request. Dealing with the loyal opposition is a skill required of people on both sides of an issue. Fortunately, most boards do not need to call on this skill often, but it is wise to be prepared.

This question about the dissenting board member is a good reminder that people are people and that governance requires trust, diplomacy, respect for differing points of view, and all the virtues of community living.

✓

SUGGESTED ACTION STEPS

1. Ask for a 10-minute discussion on how well the board understands and accepts the principles outlined in this chapter. How would they amend them?

2. Do board members sometimes persist in opposing legitimate board actions? If so, the chief executive and the board chair should discuss who should do what, how, and when.

Part III

Selection and Development of Board Members

19

What should a board development plan include?

"We're so busy improving the organization that we never focus on ourselves."

What is the reason for a board development plan? To be honest, many boards never get around to putting a plan into writing. They may carry out some pieces of board development, such as an orientation program for new members, but they don't think about the whole menu of possibilities for cultivating, selecting, training, and motivating board members. Boards — and organizations — deserve better.

A written plan will reinforce the idea that board development is a year-round, ongoing process consisting of interconnected activities. The plan should spell out what happens, who is responsible, and when the activity occurs. Some boards establish a month-by-month timeline as a reminder of which steps to do when throughout the year. A comprehensive board development plan might be only two pages long, but it should incorporate the following elements:

- *Create a governance committee.* A governance committee may be created by expanding the role of your nominating committee to embrace board orientation, and continuing training and evaluation.

- *Start educating potential board members* during the cultivation phase. One way to introduce candidates to the culture of the board is by inviting them to attend a board or committee meeting.

- *Organize an orientation.* No matter how diligently candidates have been prepared for their future role, nothing replaces formal orientation for new members. Organize a session that lasts a few hours or half a day and then continue the orientation throughout their first year using different methods and tools, such as a board mentor.

- *Develop a board reference book.* A well-organized four-inch three-ring binder will serve as a board member's memory and reference to anything he or she needs to know about the organization and his or her role as a board member. It should include all legal documents, financial data, the organization's strategic framework, and other board-related information.

- *Establish a mentoring system.* Many boards include mentoring in their orientation program to provide individual support to a new board member and guide him or her through the process. Mentors also help new board members learn about board culture, something they couldn't learn from reviewing documents.

- *Hold an annual board retreat.* Most boards can benefit from an annual retreat simply to strengthen relationships and focus on future challenges, but retreats are also useful in refreshing board members' understanding of their responsibilities and working out a critical issue of strategic importance.

- *Conduct periodic self-assessments.* By engaging in self-evaluation, board members are able to look at their own accomplishments within their peer group and judge whether they have reached their objectives. A good time to evaluate the performance of board members and officers is before re-election.

The entire board should adopt the board development plan, assigning clear authority for each step. Some boards create a board development or a governance committee to lead and coordinate the process, but the nominating committee may also assume this responsibility. The chief executive may participate in selecting and nurturing potential board members and in the orientation process, but primary responsibility for building the board and improving its effectiveness rests with board members themselves.

SUGGESTED ACTION STEPS

1. Try to add up the hours your board or its committees have devoted to the basic board development activities mentioned in this chapter. Are you satisfied?

2. Pinpoint the activity you believe will bring the most important short-term results. Develop a plan for concentrating on improvement in that area.

20

How can a membership organization build an effective board?

"The board doesn't have the freedom to choose its own members."

Board members are selected in a variety of ways, raising an important reminder: It is far too simple to assume all boards are alike. True, there are principles that seem to work most of the time for most boards. But this question—how board members are selected in membership organizations — focuses on a significant difference.

A formal membership organization is a nonprofit that grants its members specific rights to participate in its internal affairs. These rights are established in the articles of incorporation and defined in more detail in the bylaws. In a membership organization, the members typically elect the board. This process is very similar to the democratic process by which we elect members to school boards, state legislatures, the United States Congress, and the like. The people who have an interest in, and may be affected by, a group of decision makers should have the right to select those important people. That is a difficult position to argue against.

Many of us belong to such organizations. At intervals specified in the organization's bylaws, we receive a mail ballot for board members and officers. We read short biographies of the candidates and are asked to vote for a certain number of people. The ballot may be uncontested—with the same number of candidates as open positions — or contested — with more candidates than open positions. We may know none of the nominees, or we may have heard of a few. The process is like voting a proxy ballot for the directors of a multinational corporation.

As a member of these organizations, we feel involved when we send in our mail ballots. But as students of governance, we always wonder whether the current board members feel they could do a better job of adding to their number. If there are more candidates than there are positions, we also wonder why any organization would want to present a slate of candidates — all important volunteers — knowing some are going to be voted "losers" by their peers.

Membership organizations have their own form of politics. For example, a young person who volunteers in a large environmental organization that has local, regional, and national boards might aspire to be on the national board some day. He or she attends meetings, writes an article for the journal, runs for the local board, gets to know various members of the national board, and visits the national headquarters so the staff knows of his or her commitment. If the volunteer aspires to further serve the organization, he or she can ask friends to contact the national board's nominating committee, and he or she may end up on the ballot.

Many organizations with elected boards hold an election at the annual meeting of hundreds, even thousands, of members. A nominating committee presumably has worked hard to develop a slate of people it feels will bring balance and expertise to the board. The bylaws make it easy to have a quorum (for example, "those members present and voting"), and the whole election takes two minutes. Perhaps only three were nominated to fill three positions. The process comes close to being a self-perpetuating board, but the larger membership still has the right to object to the slate and, although difficult, promote someone other than those on the nominating committee's ballot. In such a situation, group dynamics may present a challenge.

With elected boards, there is always the potential for a popularity contest, a lack of diversity, and less mutual accountability. Developing an effective elected board requires attention to a few details that are unique to membership organizations:

- *Board members must see the organization as an entity, not as an agent for their particular constituents.* The needs of the national organization must always take precedence over the needs of a particular chapter or group represented by a board member. Avoid setting strict representational quotas or using the board election to repay political favors. Elected board members should be able to leave their personal and professional agendas at the boardroom door.

- *Cast a wide net when seeking nominees.* The nominating committee must take its job seriously, conducting an aggressive and open search throughout the organization for committed and qualified potential board members. It must understand the qualities of a good board member and be able to assess the characteristics required at a particular moment to maximize the effectiveness of the board's composition. Leadership succession planning is important, too, to ensure a pool of board candidates.

- *Present an uncontested slate to the membership.* If the nominating committee does its homework thoroughly, involving the membership in the recruitment and cultivation process, it should be able to narrow the slate of candidates to the best people for the job. Members can still make write-in nominations or nominations from the floor, of course.

SUGGESTED ACTION STEPS

1. Schedule a board discussion and critique of the nomination and selection process.

2. If even a few board members raise the need for change, appoint a task force to study and report on how other membership organizations approach this process.

21

What is the chief executive's role in board recruitment?

"I've always thought the chief executive should put anyone on the board he wants."

More than a few nonprofit board members, particularly business owners, think the board should be made up only of people the chief executive chooses. That's the way many small businesses work. The familiar rationale is "We've always done it that way." When pushed to explain further, it usually turns out that this practice started under the visionary founder, and now, three chief executives later, it continues.

It's true that many chief executives would like to choose the board members. Yet others say "When I arrived, I assumed the board selected its own members, but I was told to do that." What is acceptable practice, and why?

The board must own the responsibility to improve itself, and that includes taking the lead in recruiting new members. In fact, recruitment requires a collaborative effort of the board and the chief executive, with the board leading the process. Here are some reasons to follow this principle:

- *Continuity.* Boards provide history and continuity; chief executives come and go.

- *Commitment.* When board members are involved in recruitment, they are committed to helping the colleagues they select become successful at board service.

- *Accountability.* When the board includes a broader group than personal friends, the chief executive will be more accountable.

- *Better governance.* Cultivating, recruiting, and selecting board members requires deep thinking about the board's needs and often stimulates the board to deal with important issues it might have overlooked.

A board-oriented chief executive is encouraged, not threatened, by a strong board. But building the board's strength and effectiveness takes careful, conscious effort by the chief executive, beginning with board recruitment. It is appropriate for the chief executive to play these key roles:

- Help the board draft appropriate criteria for board membership.

- Be engaged in identifying candidates along with other staff and board members.

- Nurture the interest of potential board members.

- Consult with the board during the recruitment process.

- Brief candidates on the organization and the nonprofit sector in general.

- Follow up the board's election with a welcome call or letter and an orientation program.

Successful chief executives have considerable influence in selecting board members, but they do not own the process. Board members who have confidence in their chief executives often want to delegate as much of this hard work as they can. Resist this temptation for the long-term health of the board.

Should a chief executive have veto power over nominees? Few boards elect someone the chief executive has good reason to oppose. Consider the objection discreetly; it doesn't help to put it in writing because it will be misinterpreted. Paying attention to the chief executive's concerns may be important to the harmony and effectiveness of the board.

✅

SUGGESTED ACTION STEPS

1. Discuss your current board board member selection process. Some board members may not know what it is.

2. If the selection process is not a balanced partnership between the board and the chief executive, use some of the points in this chapter to write a workable plan.

3. Interview the three newest board members to learn their opinions about the process and their suggestions for improvement.

22

How can we recruit better, more active board members?

"I agreed to serve because of my friend Lloyd, but I don't go to many meetings."

Can you envision one of your board members saying this to a friend? We are amazed at how many people are asked to serve on a board without much knowledge, much commitment, or much expectation. With an estimated 15 million nonprofit board members in the United States, how many do you feel are the kind their organizations would most like to have?

A good way to respond to this question is "How would you like to be recruited?" We ask that because, over the years, this seems to be a maxim of nonprofit governance: The seriousness with which a board member is recruited and selected is directly proportional to the seriousness with which a board member fulfills his or her role.

How do we get good people to serve? Here is a strategy that includes five phases:

1. Define the board member's job.

Be very specific in writing a one- to two-page job description that suits the organization at this point in its life cycle. The generic roles listed in Chapter 2 are helpful for people who are unfamiliar with nonprofit board service, but prospective board members will also want to know about how this board defines its job. Remember that the responsibilities of the board as a governing body are different from the individual responsibilities of each board member.

Discuss the expectations related to each of the three hats a board member wears (governance, implementation, and volunteer). In addition to setting policy, is a board member expected to give much time as a volunteer with the organization? Do you expect, as you should, every board member to be a donor of record every year? How many committee assignments and committee meetings are expected of each board member? How will a board member's performance be evaluated?

2. Agree on the profile of the future board.

The board should describe what the "dream team" it envisions will look like in a few years. For example, describe minimums, maximums, or percentages for whatever characteristics are important for your organization. These could include age, gender, and minority representation, as well as lay versus professional, rural versus urban, and other demographic variables. The profile should be unique to your organization's current stage of development.

3. Develop qualifications for serving.

The values of the organization and its board members can be translated into a useful tool to evaluate the strengths of the current board and focus the board's thinking about characteristics sought in future members (see Figure 6). To some, completing this profile can be threatening. But if you are committed to excellence, you want to build a team of people who bring a balanced array of specialized talents and skills to the collective effort.

After the board member profile is created by the board development (or nominating) committee and approved by the entire board, it can be used to identify current or projected gaps in the desired experience and qualifications of board members. For example, the board could see that Frank will rotate off the board in one year so the board should seek a new member who has Frank's expertise.

Some groups rate individuals on a scale of one to five if the qualification lends itself to that technique. Of course, ratings should be kept confidential, but a blank copy of this profile is helpful in the next phase of recruiting. The profile should fit your organization, so use this one only as a sample.

4. Adopt a plan to identify and nurture prospects.

So far, you have identified expectations and qualifications to guide recruiting the best people for the board. Using these two written documents, develop a simple action plan to start a list of people who might fit the board. The identification process is ongoing and should involve all board members. The best sources of prospects are the organization's own board and staff. Major donors, friends in other nonprofits, and even your neighbor might think of a name or two. Selecting new board members is not complicated, but it is deliberate work.

Let's assume you build a list of six or eight people who seem to meet most qualifications. Before asking them to join the board, find meaningful ways to involve them as volunteers. They might serve on a task force, host a luncheon, or give feedback on a draft document based on their expertise. If a person is not responsive at this level, what could you expect if he or she joined the board?

Gradually extend the prospective board member's involvement in the organization. Eventually, if he or she is not yet a donor, ask for a contribution. If you ask more than once but still get no response, beware. The person is probably not yet ready for board membership.

Figure 6

Board Member Profile

DESIRED CHARACTERISTICS	CURRENT MEMBERS		PROSPECTIVE MEMBERS	
MEMBER:	1	2	3	4
ALL MEMBERS SHOULD HAVE THESE CHARACTERISTICS:				
Demonstrated interest before nomination				
Donor of record in last year				
Some experience in our area of service				
Board service supported by family				
Able to attend meetings; give 8 to 10 days a year				
Known as good group decisionmaker				
Other?				
EACH MEMBER SHOULD HAVE ONE OR MORE OF THESE CHARACTERISTICS:				
Recognized community leader				
Prior experience on nonprofit boards				
Knowledge of nonprofit law				
Knowledge of nonprofit fund-raising				
Specialized knowledge of one mission/program area				
Helps balance the board in terms of gender				
Helps balance the board in terms of age				
Helps balance the board in terms of ethnicity				
Experience in marketing our services				
Good mediator of group disagreements				
Knowledge of land use and facilities management				
Experience in dealing with local government				
Has network of donor prospects				
Leadership in another organization important to us				
Other:				

5. Be rigorous about the nomination process.

The board development committee is now ready to consider a slate of known talent to fill the most critical needs on the board. Look at balance. Determine who could be groomed for a key leadership role down the road, knowing who is likely to leave the board. Agree on who should meet with each highly rated prospect.

We suggest that you ask these prospects whether they are willing to be considered. Invite them to read the job description and the list of desired qualifications. Point out which qualifications you feel they have, and ask how they believe they meet others. Offer to lend them copies of the bylaws and board policy manual for review.

When a nominee shows interest, consider some other preliminary orientation steps. The chart in Figure 7 lists some things prospective board members should know. Take the time now for a thorough explanation of what board service involves so later there are no surprises. When you inform prospective members thoroughly, they develop high expectations for board service.

Reference checks are appropriate at this stage in the nominating process. You wouldn't think of hiring a staff member without consulting references, and we believe board member selection is at least as important a decision.

6. Take board election and new member orientation seriously.

This last step is a key investment in effective governance. The actual election and the welcoming event can be memorable for new board members. So will efforts to help them learn the ropes during their early months on the board. These first impressions will last a long time. Just before the new member's first official meeting, and in the few weeks following, continue the orientation checklist in Figure 7. Some items might require the board member to take the initiative. Others usually will be up to the chair, board development committee chair, or chief executive. New board members who are welcomed to the board in this way will take their responsibilities seriously. The learning curve is shortened, and new members soon feel knowledgeable enough to participate actively in board business. They will want future board members to be selected and oriented with as much care as they were. Once you start this tradition, you begin to perpetuate a model for responsible governance and effective board operations.

Recruiting good board members is only the beginning. To keep them informed, involved, and motivated, the board should continually evaluate itself and commit to effective board practices. That's why we can't stop writing with this chapter!

Figure 7

New Board Member Orientation Checklist

ITEM	BEFORE ELECTION	SOON AFTER ELECTION	BY WHOM?	WHEN?
1. Organization's history and mission	X			
2. Role and expectations of board members	X			
3. Bylaws, budget, current members	X			
4. Strategic plan, major goals	X			
5. Programs and staff overview	X			
6. Facility visit and staff introductions	X	X		
7. Briefing on program strategies and results		X		
8. Introduction to committees and advisory groups		X		
9. Committee assignments and orientation		X		
10. Calendar of meetings and events		X		
11. Field visits (if applicable)		X		
12. Library of organizational information		X		
13. Review of audits, insurance, contracts		X		
14. Other:				
15. Other:				

✔

SUGGESTED ACTION STEPS

1. Let board members read this chapter and give feedback on whether this approach is reasonable and practical. If not, ask them for better ideas for recruiting quality board members.

2. Before working too hard on recruiting more board members, think about how many board members you really need (see Chapter 10). Then ask how you can deal with inactive board members (see Chapter 30).

3. Brainstorm with board members about the elements of a good orientation program. Some experienced members will discover they need to be brought up to date in a few areas.

23

Should board members be compensated?

"I don't get paid to be on this board, but I feel more than compensated for my time."

Serving on a nonprofit board is usually a volunteer commitment. Offering compensation for board service raises issues that need to be studied carefully. There are circumstances where reasonable compensation is acceptable, but it is always critical that board service neither leads to personal financial gain nor violates the public trust.

DETERMINING WHEN COMPENSATION IS APPROPRIATE

Although nonprofit board service is usually a volunteer activity, reasonable fees for service are permissible if the bylaws state so or the majority of the board so determines. However, such compensation is rare. According to *The Nonprofit Governance Index*, a survey conducted by BoardSource (formerly the National Center for Nonprofit Boards) in conjunction with Stanford University, only 2 percent of the more than 1,300 organizations surveyed compensated their board members for the time spent on board business; for the majority of those that did, the fees were nominal.

Board compensation is more common in complex nonprofits, such as health care systems or large foundations. Many organizations believe a fee is appropriate when the responsibilities of board members are particularly time-consuming or when legal requirements make the service unusually demanding. Also, compensation can make it possible for individuals of very limited financial means to participate in board service.

According to the basic tenets of nonprofit law, directors and officers should not make any pecuniary (monetary) profit from the organization and they should not receive personal financial benefit from their association with the organization. Paying a fee in specific circumstances can be defended, but fees that are out of scale with the market price of that good or service are always unacceptable. Excessive compensation can be a cause for a fine or for the organization to lose its tax-exempt status.

To avoid even a perception of personal gain, the board might want to have compensation determinations made by a task force of appropriate outsiders or a board committee whose members lack conflict of interest with respect to the arrangement. Here are some common situations organizations may encounter with their boards:

1. Reimbursement of expenses

Traveling to a distant board meeting can become a major expense. Not every board member has equal financial capacity to absorb those costs. But paying for plane tickets, hotel accommodations, and meals can become a substantial expense for the nonprofit — even if the total amount compensated is limited. This is a policy issue that needs to be clarified for potential new board members. It is acceptable to make reimbursement available, but a policy should be established by the board. Many organizations ask that board members absorb travel costs as a way to support the organization. Board service, however, should not cause personal economic hardship. According to the BoardSource (formerly the National

Center for Nonprofit Boards) survey, 13 percent of the respondents' organizations regularly reimbursed board members for their expenses and another 13 percent did so if board members specifically requested it.

2. Business relationships with board members

It is not uncommon that board members recommend their own business services to the organization on whose board they serve. It is not inappropriate for a nonprofit organization to have business relationships with board members. But it is extremely important to follow appropriate and ethical procedures before this kind of a relationship is established. A conflict-of-interest policy that requires board members to annually disclose personal and professional affiliations assures the organization is treating potential conflicts of interest with appropriate diligence. The organization needs to openly seek bids to procure services, keeping in mind what is best for the organization must be the determining factor. Sometimes a board member is willing to provide services at a discount. In any case, it is important to be able to document that the final decision was made in the best interests of the nonprofit and that the board was aware of the potential conflict.

3. Board members wearing two hats

Often during the beginning phase in the life of an organization, the board may have two functions: It acts as the governing body while at the same time fulfilling the duties of staff. In some arts organizations, board members also act as directors or producers. In some hospitals, board members may also be physicians. This situation may complicate the issue of accountability. Being compensated for staff activities while simultaneously serving as a volunteer overseer of the organization may create confusion between the two responsibilities. Board members may want to consider making a tough choice and determining which activity they prefer to pursue — being part of the staff or the board. Another option is to excuse him- or herself from some decisions. The chair or the chief executive may need to gently remind board members of their conflicting interests.

4. Donors' expectations

Funders or individual donors generally expect their contributions to go to programs and services. The board should take into account possible reactions from funders and donors before it begins accepting compensation for board service.

Each compensation situation needs to be assessed thoroughly to avoid any improprieties. Boards need to be vigilant about creating appropriate policies and seeing that they are implemented. Tying board service to monetary benefits can cloud board members' judgment by tempting them to make decisions based on personal interest rather than what is best for the organization.

Each board member should answer the question: How does my commitment change if I am paid for the service? Sometimes the time and monetary burden can be too demanding without any compensation. In that case, before accepting the commitment or before lowering the standards of promised involvement, it is important to communicate these concerns to the chair of the board. The honorable solution may be for the board member to rotate off the board.

SUGGESTED ACTION STEPS

1. If you are considering compensating your board members, do some research to find out how many nonprofits in your area pay board members for their board work and how much board members receive.

2. Because board members are looking for personal, intangible rewards, take 10 minutes of a board meeting to talk about the adequacy of those rewards.

24

How should the board reflect the diversity of our culture?

"As I look around the table, all of us look pretty much alike, think alike, and agree on most things."

Diversity is a topic with many dimensions. We believe it is important to call attention here to its importance in the governance process. We like Jennifer M. Rutledge's observation about inclusiveness in her book *Building Board Diversity* published by BoardSource (formerly the National Center for Nonprofit Boards): "On an inclusive board, individual board members contribute an array of talents, skills, and interests that result from their own experiences and origins. Collectively, the board is enriched by diversity, as individuals take advantage of their differences to work successfully together on behalf of the organization."[1]

Boards have different reasons and approaches for bringing a diverse group of people together. What most try to do is attract board members who are among the moral owners of the organization. There may be important reasons for a board to include more women, for example, or people from different racial backgrounds. For other boards, diversity may mean including both professional and lay people, or rural and urban residents, or people from other regions of the country. Making inclusiveness a goal builds confidence that the board and the organization are committed to serving their constituency.

One of the most important reasons a board should strive for diversity, we believe, is to gain a variety of views. Otherwise, why should a board be larger than three or four people? To have this kind of diversity requires a board that welcomes different points of view and a chair who leads the dialogue in such a way that a broad spectrum of ideas and perspectives is presented and considered. Of course, once a board has spoken with one voice on policy, those holding contrary opinions must be loyal to the majority. This attitude will follow when the discussion is open and no one feels penalized for voicing what might be an unpopular view.

Another motivation for board diversity is to give the board a way to link with its constituents. On some national boards, it would be impossible to represent every group and background. You would have to be willing to have a board of 100 or more people. So the board needs to ask itself what, other than full representation on the board, enables it to stay in touch with its constituents. Reporting to them is one way of communicating. Listening — through surveys, focus groups, or open forums with board members at annual conventions — is even more important. By listening well, a board can be informed of the broad range of its constituents' values, opinions, needs, and hopes.

While all of these ideas are useful, many readers may say we are not addressing the issue. The issue, they would say, is to reduce the homogeneity of nonprofit boards. And while that is the goal, we offer some points to consider as that goal is pursued.

- Some boards simply float along, nominating people board members know, leading to a board that looks fairly homogeneous. No one has ever made the case for working harder to find people who would bring a broader variety of experience and views. These boards need to address this issue frankly as part of the recruitment and nominating process, look at how inclusiveness could strengthen the organization, and decide on the best strategy.

- There is no shortage of outstanding women, minority, and younger prospective board members. There is no excuse for not including them when other board qualifications are met.

- A board should beware of tokenism, which is not a serious attempt to reflect greater diversity.

- It is unfair and dangerous to expect one person to be the "representative" of a population that has traditionally been left out. No one person can adequately reflect the viewpoints of an entire group.

- Having a more diverse board does not lessen the obligation of the entire board to learn and reflect the variety of views that need to be considered in policymaking.

Keeping these principles in mind, and appreciating the increasing diversity of our population, we believe it is appropriate for most boards representing broad constituencies to intentionally and affirmatively seek board members from groups that have lacked representation on the board. Some good interim moves might be inviting non-board members to sit on advisory councils or certain board committees, or having joint meetings with leaders from unrepresented sectors. These efforts will build the relationships and networks a board needs to find good board members (and staff) from new groups.

Diversity and inclusiveness are important issues in building quality boards for the next century, especially in the United States. We need to act positively, not defensively or reluctantly, in moving ahead. William G. Bowen, an expert on both corporate and nonprofit boards, sets the right tone:

> For many organizations, no problem is more difficult at the
> present time than finding the best way of including on
> governing boards members of previously excluded groups,
> especially racial minorities. It can be tempting to adopt the

easy approach of earmarking positions (the "black seat" on a board), but this seems to me patronizing, potentially very dangerous, and an inadequate response to the opportunity to enrich a board by recruiting outstanding individuals of diverse backgrounds and persuasions.[2]

We hope you will face this important topic with courage and honesty. We need more models of how to change in this area. This requires humility and openness.

SUGGESTED ACTION STEPS

1. Have an open discussion about how well the board reflects the diversity of its constituencies.

2. Develop a list of desired qualifications for board membership, including the need for people of different ages, genders, religious beliefs, races, professional experiences, and so forth (see Chapter 22).

3. Strategize how best to identify and recruit people who will bring a healthy new ingredient to the governance process.

4. Ask whether new board members from diverse backgrounds are fully involved in the work of the board. Make the effort to listen to their perceptions of the organization and the directions they think it should go, and take the opportunity to learn from them.

---

1. Jennifer M. Rutledge, *Building Board Diversity* (Washington, DC: National Center for Nonprofit Boards [now BoardSource], 1994), pp. 7–8.

2. William G. Bowen, *Inside the Boardroom: Governance by Directors and Trustees* (New York: John Wiley & Sons, 1994), p. 48.

25

What does a prospective board member need to know?

"I was told 'It's a great group, and it won't take much time.' But now I know differently."

Too few people ask the right questions (or any questions) before taking on the significant responsibility of board membership. Have you ever received this call? "We voted last night to elect you to our board. Will you accept?" The caller then often goes on to say, "This won't take a lot of your time. It's just a bunch of good people who enjoy being together."

Board service involves a lot more than that. The board has legal and moral responsibility for the organization. A governing board role should not be viewed as honorary or advisory or "just helping out my friend, the chief executive." Board membership should be a serious decision.

We suggest you ask at least 10 questions before agreeing to serve on a board:

1. What is the mission of the organization?

The mission should drive the whole organization. It should be clear and in writing. Policies and actions flowing from that mission should be evident. Can you support it? It is best if the organization's mission actually touches one of your personal passions. Can you give your best to ensure the mission's success? Halfhearted support does not help an organization.

2. Who are the leaders of the organization?

Do you know them? Do you respect their reputations? As a new board member, you will discover a strong board chair, or more typically the chief executive officer, often has enormous influence over board decisions. If you do not know these people, get to know them first. If you do not respect them, then service on the board will be difficult.

3. What is the financial condition of the organization?

Almost every nonprofit board struggles with finances. Ask for the last external audit. Also ask to see the latest budget, revenue and expenditure statement, cash flow budget, and balance sheet. Although you should contribute to the financial stability of any organization on whose board you serve, you need to join a board with your eyes wide open. Service on a board where financial problems consume every meeting is not very fulfilling.

4. What is the board member's job description?

Unfortunately, few organizations have good job descriptions. Without a common understanding of what their roles are, board members can waste time and effort and become frustrated because of differing assumptions about what they should be doing. The issue is often postured as the role of the board vs. the role of the staff. See Part V of this book for more on this. The point here is to find out whether the current board agrees about its collective role and the role of individual board members.

5. How long is my term?

Most boards elect members for terms of two or three years. Some, to encourage rotation and invite new perspectives, limit the number of consecutive terms. How long is your term? Is it a full term, or are you completing an unexpired term? Traditionally, is re-election essentially automatic? How many terms is it possible to serve? Will you have a reasonable opportunity to politely decline re-election when your term is up, or will that cause hard feelings you are unwilling to endure?

6. How much of my time will be required in a normal year?

Most boards require the equivalent of a minimum of five to eight days per year. Many board members give much more, depending on how much and how often they volunteer for nonboard activities. The expected time commitment includes preparation for board and committee meetings, the meetings themselves, travel, assignments, and special projects. Boards that meet outside your city may meet less often, but the travel time will increase. Some board members need to take time off to make all the meetings. Can you commit to the time required?

7. How many meetings will I be expected to attend, and when are they?

Meetings may take up less time than other responsibilities. But you may have standing commitments that conflict with an already-determined schedule of board meetings. Or, if the board always meets on Saturdays, you may be unwilling to take that additional time away from your personal life. Committee meeting dates usually are flexible and are not set far in advance. Board meeting dates should be set a year in advance. Consider also the major events the organization sponsors and which ones board members are expected to attend.

A related question is, "Do I enjoy group meetings?" Many people agree to serve on a board out of some charitable motivation, only later to acknowledge, "I hate sitting in meetings."

8. Who pays for my expenses as a board member?

If no out-of-town travel is required, expenses for board service can be minimal. But they can be considerable if you have to fly to a few meetings, drive long distances, or stay in a hotel. Meals, long-distance calls, and other miscellaneous items contribute to the expense.

In order to be able to attract board members from different socio-economic levels, nonprofit organization should have a policy on reimbursing expenses. Not having this policy can often deter good people from serving on the board. Many organizations assume all board members are willing and able to assume their own expenses — often a false assumption, but a traditional one. It is important to be clear about the board's expectations and be willing to accept them. If you do incur personal expenses in official service as a board member of a tax-exempt charitable organization, you can list them on your personal income tax return as a charitable contribution.

9. Are all board members expected to be donors?

We recall many board members who assumed that staff raised funds and others were the major donors, only to discover at the second or third meeting that board members were expected to come up with a significant portion of the annual budget. In fact, some boards depend on their members so much financially that you would not be elected unless you were viewed as a potential major donor.

Be clear so you are not surprised down the road. We believe every board member should be a donor of record for his or her organization every year.

The extent of the expectation is what you need to investigate before joining the board. In addition to being donors, most board members are expected to open doors to friends and acquaintances who might be contributors. Are you willing to do this? It is a good question that tests your overall level of commitment to the organization's mission.

10. What are my motivations for serving as a board member?

Once you've gathered all this information, your own motivations will begin to emerge. By now you know it will take more time and money than you might have expected. You will be aware of some of the problems the organization faces. It looks like board service entails more than just the honor of being asked.

You should not serve out of a sense of obligation or to look good among your friends. Board membership requires more than that. We should look more to what we can cheerfully give than to what we will gain from serving on a board. You are right to ask, "How will service here help me grow and allow me to contribute what I do best?" Few volunteer board members are good contributors who serve out of guilt or from a superficial willingness to respond to the friend who extended the opportunity. For board service to be a priority in your life, however, you need to consider the potential for personal enrichment.

A thought for current board members and chief executives: Take the opportunity to make your organization look better when it recruits new board members by collecting answers to these questions in advance. We believe in truth in advertising. Be vulnerable in telling as much about your organization as you can to someone you are considering for the board. Ask the person to review material before discussing possible service. A candidate's diligence in actually reading and discussing the material is a clue to whether you were right in thinking he or she was a good possibility. Your candidate will be impressed by the thoroughness of your recruitment and screening. We repeat that a board member's effort often reflects the seriousness of the nomination process. We all want to feel that we deserved the privilege of serving.

SUGGESTED ACTION STEPS

1. Find as many answers to our questions as possible. Do not say "yes" until you have. If you are a board member, do you have all the answers?

2. Ask to meet with the chief executive alone so you can ask probing questions about the organization and about his or her goals, dreams, and frustrations.

3. Talk with two or three current board members about what they enjoy about serving and what they view as the board's upcoming challenges.

4. Ask whether your family will support you in this assignment, because it will affect them to some extent.

26

Is it right to acknowledge personal motives for serving on a board?

"I have three young daughters, so I hoped to learn a lot about teen pregnancy by serving on this board."

Should a board member have personal motives for serving? Of course. Most do. All board members have motives — some good and some not so good — that must be considered. Personal motives may affect selection, assignment, relationship building, and evaluation. We hope our exploration of this issue will open up some new ways for board members, especially the chair, and the chief executive, to keep the board out of trouble and raise the satisfaction level.

Our interest in this topic was piqued by Alvin F. Zander, a scholar in group dynamics. His research is quite clear: "People who become members of a governing board bring personal motives with them to the board. They want, for example, to find friends, develop skills, pick up specific information, win approval, attain prestige, or engage in activities the board sponsors."[1] The trick, of course, is to identify these motives and leverage

125

Is it right to acknowledge personal motives for serving on a board?

them for the good of the organization. When a board member's individual goals for service do not complement the values and mission of the organization, problems can develop. But when individual motivations and goals are complementary, the board member will excel and the organization will benefit.

Because this question is very personal, we will make you aware of some general principles. You will have to apply them to the individuals who are members of, or being considered for, your board.

- *Recruit wisely.* In Chapter 22 we discussed the importance of careful recruitment and selection. It is appropriate to ask prospective members, "What three or four things would you hope to gain personally from serving on our board?" Perhaps a candidate has not put it into words, but we all know that our busy lives require us to evaluate all facets of a potential new commitment. Now is the time to acknowledge that all board members have self-oriented motives for serving. Perhaps the prospective member can give some feedback that allows you to assess whether his or her expectations are reasonable for your board.

- *Provide pre-election orientation.* We believe in providing full information to a candidate prior to the formal invitation to serve (see Figure 7, Chapter 22). This is a good time to share the history, mission, and culture of your organization. Maybe the candidate will decide that his or her own expectations will not be met by serving on the board. If the candidate declines to be nominated on the basis of this realization, you have prevented a potentially difficult situation for the candidate and the board.

- *Have a board discussion of hopes and expectations.* From time to time, ideally in a retreat setting, it can be productive to open the topic of personal motives for discussion by the full board. The process could be small groups, a written survey with a report by a neutral person, or an open discussion. Boards in which there is a great deal of trust can often deal effectively with questions about motives. Perhaps the conversation will allow one board member to gently suggest to another,

"It may be unreasonable for you to fulfill that personal expectation on our board." Or a comment may lead the group to decide that a personal expectation is laudable and seek ways to meet it. Perhaps the whole board would benefit, and the result would be more effective, involved, motivated governance. This is an opportunity for the board to get to a new level of communication and understanding.

What do we mean? Here is one example: A medical doctor serving on an inner city social services board expresses his hope that someday he can volunteer time with certain families served by the organization, but he doesn't want to rush things. That kind of comment could easily trigger the idea that the organization challenge many doctors and dentists to volunteer as well. Another example is a new board member who says she wants to learn from this board because she has just been asked to chair another board and she feels unprepared. It may turn out that many board members serve on other boards, so this board could be a model of board excellence that could benefit other organizations.

It is not only right to acknowledge personal motivations but by doing so, it can open up a whole new level of vision and energy.

SUGGESTED ACTION STEPS

1. Ask board members to list their reasons for serving on the board. Do they have realistic expectations that match the mission of the organization and the roles and responsibilities of board members?

2. At a board meeting, the chair could ask a willing volunteer to explain his or her expectations and motivations for serving. This question might open up a good dialogue.

---

1. Alvin F. Zander, *Making Boards Effective: The Dynamics of Nonprofit Governing Boards* (San Francisco, CA: Jossey-Bass, 1993), p. 11.

27

Should members of the same family serve on a board?

"This is really a small family business incorporated as a nonprofit."

This question is worth taking seriously, because mistakes related to family members on the same board can be disastrous. Generally, it is inadvisable to seat family members on the same board. There are exceptions, of course, and in cases where the practice makes sense, a clear set of policies must be put in place to address nepotism and conflict of interest. Such policies could minimize the potential for internal conflict while reassuring prospective board members, donors, government agencies, or others important to the organization that the board takes its public stewardship seriously.

One argument for the practice is to maintain a multigenerational history of major involvement and giving. For example, some nonprofit boards without term limits have benefited greatly over the years, usually including significant financial gifts, from a person who is growing older. Maybe the whole family has been involved as volunteers and donors. It would not be unusual to nurture, and then elect to the board, one of this board member's children to overlap a term or two with the parent. The assumption would be that the younger member would help sustain the family's interest for many more years. However, there should be a strong rationale for overlapping rather than sequential terms, such as passing on a family legacy or keeping continuous and secure family ties.

Occasionally, a board has a tradition of electing couples as members. This happens most often in local or regional charitable organizations—a children's home, a foster-care organization, or even an organization that provides educational programs to enhance marriage. Another situation might involve a founder who, starting to launch a vision from the kitchen table, invites the spouse to serve on the first board. While it is rare that both spouses would bring the same high level of interest and the special experience desired by the board, it is entirely possible. Boards should approach the practice of electing spouses with great care. This is especially true for small boards, which might discover that filling board slots with spouses makes it difficult to achieve diversity goals or find the skills the board needs.

Another common example is the board of a family foundation, either operating or grantmaking. Families often hope to use board membership as a way of engaging younger generations in philanthropy. This approach may work well, depending on the individuals involved. It is important to engage a few people from outside the family to bring a more objective view and a balanced perspective to the board table.

If a board decides that it wants to allow members of the same family as board members, it should acknowledge the risks and establish clear policies to address nepotism and potential conflicts of interest.

SUGGESTED ACTION STEPS

1. If your board has never faced this question, consider developing a policy before the situation arises.

2. If you do have family members on the board, seek a common understanding of the reasons for doing so and express those principles in a policy.

28

How should constituents be involved in the work of the board?

"Our problem is trying to make everyone feel represented on the board."

An organization's constituents — those people who make a difference in achieving the mission — should be involved in the work of the board. They might serve as voting members, participate through committees, or feel engaged through regular communication with the organization. A board can sort out these options by assessing what expertise, skills, and personal qualities are needed to help the board do its work. Many boards develop a board profile and revise it as needed (see Chapter 22). This process forces the question of whether, how many, and which constituents should be considered for the board.

What is a constituent? In the corporate world, these people are called stockholders, and board members are never confused about on whose behalf

131

How should constituents be involved in the work of the board?

they are making policy. In the nonprofit world, those to whom a board should feel primary accountability may be more difficult to define. Some use the term "stakeholders." John Carver refers to "moral owners" as those stakeholders on whose behalf the board is accountable to others, as distinguished from "primary beneficiaries," who are those being served.[1] Here are some examples:

- In a private school, parents are clearly among the moral owners to whom the board is accountable. Whether they are called stakeholders or constituents, the board needs parent representation. But the children are the primary beneficiaries and, in this case, unlikely candidates for board membership.

- A local theater group has many volunteers, donors, and a paying public. The board must be cognizant of them all. The volunteers and donors could be called the moral owners, while audiences are the primary beneficiaries. In this case, it makes sense to consider qualified individuals from both groups for board membership.

- Members of a state association of CPAs pay dues to their association and certainly remind the board that they are the moral owners. The association is set up to serve its members, so they are also the primary beneficiaries. The board would most likely have major representation from members.

- A community foundation has donors who entrust their money to the foundation's management and grantmaking skills. One could argue whether the donors are the moral owners and the primary beneficiaries or whether the grantees who receive foundation funds are the primary beneficiaries.

The key is for each board to define the organization's constituency and then determine how these people should be involved in the board. It is important to remember that constituent board members serve the interests of the whole organization. They are not spokespersons or watchdogs for their particular interest groups.

In membership organizations, such as trade associations, board representation is described clearly in the bylaws. The majority of the board typically is elected by the members, who are the organization's primary beneficiaries and moral owners. In nonmembership organizations, which may have self-perpetuating or appointed boards, the board should define the moral owners and develop ways to ensure their representation. Not all board members will be moral owners, however. An organization of doctors who provide volunteer medical help to developing nations will need board members from fields such as finance, fund-raising, and international development, as well as health-care professionals.

Primary beneficiaries, surely among the key stakeholders in an organization, could be elected to the board in certain cases. Colleges may have students represented on the board, but secondary schools will not. Health and social-service agencies are increasingly recruiting clients to serve on their boards.

Having constituents as voting board members is often a good practice, but getting their input can also be handled in other ways. The board can establish positive patterns of communication with people to whom the organization is accountable and find other options for them to participate. Many organizations invite key constituents to serve on board committees, task forces, or advisory groups. The board chair may write a regular column in the newsletter, or board activities may be listed on the Web site. Or the organization could hold a town-hall meeting at which the board answers questions from the community. Constituents will feel that their views are represented if they see evidence of the board's interest.

Donors are certainly worthy of consideration for board membership, with some cautions. First, some donors are enthusiastic about the organization but not interested in serving on the board. Inviting them would put them on the spot, and they may be embarrassed to say no. Instead, invite donors to engage in another volunteer project. Second, donors may not necessarily make good board members. When inviting a donor, be sure he or she fits the characteristics the board requires.

SUGGESTED ACTION STEPS

1. Agree on a definition of the organization's constituents. What level of giving would qualify a donor to be included in this category?

2. List the ways your board now links with these moral owners. Is there one additional communication tool you could add that would increase constituent involvement?

3. Have you articulated board member qualifications — based on a board profile — that will ensure adequate representation of your key constituents?

---

1. John Carver, *Boards that Make a Difference*, 2nd ed. (San Francisco, CA: Jossey-Bass, 1997).

What do we do with inactive board members?

"It is frustrating when we just barely make a quorum at most meetings."

In forums around the country, chief executives as well as board members ask us what to do about deadwood on their boards. No one likes to carry the loads of others. We don't enjoy bringing people up to speed because they miss meetings constantly. And it is not fulfilling to be part of a board where deadwood keeps the group from feeling effective.

We're not sure we like the term deadwood to describe good people, but it is correctly associated with a real problem: inactivity. While working on the front end to recruit more committed, loyal, fully participating board members, a good board also should face up to the problem of finding a gracious way out the back door for others.

Rather than allowing faithful board members to become discouraged by the inactivity of some, we suggest that the board chair pull together a few veterans to discuss the problem. Have these one or two board members lost interest? Is there a personality conflict that needs to be resolved? Is there something about the board's operations or working style that is allowing decision making to be dominated by a few? Have other priorities in life taken over? Or maybe they want off the board but don't want to appear disloyal by asking to resign. The reasons are myriad. It is best to understand them before taking action you will regret later.

When a board decides to analyze the problem of deadwood, it may mean poor selection processes were in place. In this case, the board and the individuals at issue share the problem. Be careful not to point fingers.

We suggest the following strategies for reducing inactivity and discovering ways to achieve full participation:

- *Required rotation.* Bylaw provisions that require everyone to be off the board for at least one year after a certain number of years can be highly effective. This policy allows board members a periodic freedom of choice about further service. Except in larger, more complex organizations such as universities and hospitals, six years — either two three-year terms or three two-year terms — is a good length of time before a required year off. Some board members will truly take a year off, with no demonstration of continued interest at all. That is a good sign that re-election would be a mistake for both the individual and the board. Those who want to stay involved as volunteers may be rested and ready for another tour after the required sabbatical.

- *Nonboard members on board committees.* If your bylaws allow this, some board members will more readily volunteer to leave the board as voting members if they can continue to serve on a board committee. Board membership may not be that important to these people, but they would like to help in a particular area of interest, such as strategic planning or finance. Absent such a provision, they may feel they need to be on the board in order to contribute anything.

- *Board alumni council.* In older organizations, particularly those without required term limits, a board member who is loyal to the mission and wants an ongoing affiliation stays on the governing body because there is no appropriate alternative. Some are major donors who are kept on, in spite of their inactivity, for an understandable reason. But after 20 or 30 years, or when a board member reaches a certain age, he or she is either burning out or rusting out. Forming a board member alumni council for these people makes sense. Any board member who serves more than a specified number of years is automatically eligible for life membership in this group. Once there are a dozen or so members, it may elect its own officers. Council members may be invited to board meetings as observers, and the chief executive should stay in touch with them via special communications. Honor board alumni in publications and recognize them at special events, seek their advice on key issues, and encourage them to meet for social events as they choose.

- *Attendance rule with automatic termination.* No one likes to fire a respected friend and volunteer, so some boards adopt a rule that says board members are automatically terminated following two or three unexcused absences. The trick here is defining unexcused. Usually, an excused absence simply means the board member notified the chair in advance that he or she couldn't attend a meeting. Without these advance notifications, a no-show board member would be unexcused. At some point the chair should inform the delinquent board member in writing that the board has agreed, absent an immediate request for reconsideration, that the automatic termination provision should take effect. You would be surprised at how many uninvolved board members give a sigh of relief when they get that letter. While this policy works for many boards, a formal letter of termination is seldom required.

- *Annual affirmation statement.* When you commit to a three-year term with full intent to be an active member, you are sincere. But personal situations do change. A failed business, the death of a family member, a transfer to another city—whatever the reason, board members have to look at their commitments through a different pair of glasses. What do you do? We suggest that board members routinely sign an annual affirmation statement just before the annual nominating and election process begins (see Figure 8). This statement is a good reminder of the obligations to which a board member has committed, and most do sign and return it. But it also provides an opportunity, without too much embarrassment, to respond, "My life has changed and, in all honesty, I can no longer sign for the coming year." There should be no hard feelings, because both the board and the individual benefit from this honesty.

Note that a suggested last paragraph in the affirmation statement puts the burden on the individual board member — not the board — to send a signal whenever he or she feels unable to fulfill all the expectations of board service. By including this paragraph, the board communicates that service is more than an honor. Every individual is important, and all are expected to stay active. But everyone understands that life has many priorities, and there are no hard feelings when one opts off the board. Of course, good board members can always be re-elected when their lives will allow active service again.

The familiar "Could we have lunch sometime?" can be an easy first step to take. Isn't it amazing how a good, honest, nonthreatening conversation can clear the air? Many board chairs will assume leadership in dealing with someone whom other board members begin to view as deadwood. (Some say they would rather initiate this conversation than ask someone for $5,000.) Inactive board members are not surprised that someone is concerned enough to say something. Often they have been aware (often with great guilt) of their delinquency for some time. They just didn't know how to handle the idea that they should resign. And at other times, the problem is simply a misunderstanding or a false assumption. A friendly conversation solves the problem. Usually, an agreement is made, and you either have a reactivated board member or one who feels he or she can now leave without hard feelings.

Figure 8

BOARD MEMBER ANNUAL AFFIRMATION OF SERVICE

1. I continue to be fully supportive of our mission, purpose, goals, and leadership.

2. I understand that board membership requires the equivalent of X days per year of my time, including preparation and meetings. I am able to give that time during the 12 months ahead, and I expect to attend all board and committee meetings unless I give the respective board chair advance notice of my need to be absent for good cause.

3. I intend to contribute financially to the work of our organization during the year and will help open doors to friends who may be interested in contributing to our work.

4. I have reviewed, signed, and intend to comply with our board's conflict-of-interest policy.

5. [Add other items important to your board.]

6. If anything should occur during the year that would not allow me to keep these intentions of being a positive contributor to our board, I will take the initiative to talk to the officers about a voluntary resignation to allow another to serve who is able to be fully involved.

Signed _____ Date _____

Please return your signed statement to the board secretary in the envelope provided. Thank you.

SUGGESTED ACTION STEPS

1. Take the initiative. First, see whether your concern about the inactivity of one or more board members is of concern to others. If so, discuss some alternatives with them. If a few of you have consensus on a strategy, take the board chair to lunch.

2. Read Chapter 22 again and evaluate whether the problem may be tied to the recruitment process. Fix that process to prevent future problems with inactive board members.

3. Visit with a few former board members for counsel on this issue. Their wisdom can be more easily expressed to a chief executive or board chair than some current board members.

Should individual board members be evaluated periodically?

*"I really doubt that I'm measuring up
as a member of this board."*

Everyone likes to know how he or she is doing on any assignment. Board members are no exception. But nonprofit boards are notorious for neglecting evaluation of any kind — the chief executive, programs, the board as a whole, or individual board members. Evaluation is critical to individual and organizational effectiveness. Here we offer some suggestions for making board member evaluation a regular and productive part of board service.

The first priority in evaluation is for the board to evaluate itself as a group: Are we structured well? Is our role clear? Do we focus on policy? This obligation is ongoing; we described it in Chapter 9. But good governance doesn't happen without some kind of sensitive evaluation of those doing the governing. A board committed to evaluation will usually want to evaluate themselves as individuals.

But how should they do it? And who should do it? These are sticky questions even when a board agrees that individual board members should be evaluated. The following suggestions were structured to encourage you to view board member evaluation as just as important as staff evaluation.

1. Predetermine the criteria.

Your policies should include a job description for the board, expectations of board members, and a profile of the desired qualities of new board members (see Chapter 22), all approved by the board. Board members should know these reference points for evaluation before their election. Some specific areas of evaluation might include

- attendance at meetings;
- study and preparation for meetings;
- willingness to make constructive comments in building consensus;
- loyalty to board decisions, even when the member disagrees;
- contribution of special expertise that others cannot provide;
- donor of record each year at an appropriate level;
- assistance in fund-raising from other sources; and
- representation of the organization in the broader community.

BoardSource (formerly the National Center for Nonprofit Boards) has useful self-assessment tools for individual board members as well as for the board as a whole.

2. Assign the evaluation task.

A subgroup of the board, usually the board development committee, should facilitate the process. Evaluation fits with the committee's other tasks of nominating board members for election or re-election, orienting new members, and planning board education activities.

3. Create a consistent process.

When evaluation is routine rather than provoked by a crisis or uproar from a few, the task is less emotional and builds credibility. Because some board members usually end their terms each year, an evaluation will be useful in determining whether an individual should be re-elected. Evaluations occurring at the same time each year make sense to us.

4. Include self-evaluation.

Since the purpose of board member evaluation is to improve individual performance — and thus the performance of the board itself — self-evaluation is a good part of the process. Some boards use a simple format asking people to rate themselves on ten items or so using a scale of one to five. Others use an annual affirmation statement as part of this annual process (see Chapter 29), but this statement addresses commitment rather than effectiveness.

5. Consider peer evaluation.

Many organizations find peer evaluation a useful assessment and motivational tool. If you use a fairly simple process, each board member could be asked to evaluate all of his or her peers as part of the annual evaluation. A one-page summary instrument should do, perhaps a matrix listing all board members in the first column and eight to ten evaluation items in the remaining columns. The exact "scores" are not as important as letting the group identify poor performers as a basis for working with them to improve or giving the nominating process reason for not recommending re-election.

6. Maintain confidentiality.

Only the board committee conducting the evaluation should see all the responses. Committee members should discuss their own views in light of the self-evaluation and peer evaluation. This information should be reported only in very general terms to the whole board, obviously mentioning no one by name.

7. Provide individual feedback.

For some board members, a confidential phone call from the committee chair satisfies the desire to know how well he or she is doing in the eyes of others. For others, the self-evaluation itself will suffice. Remember that feedback should be based on criteria known to and applied to every board member.

8. Leverage the information.

The evaluating group now has very useful information to help it develop a better description of board member expectations, a stronger orientation program for new board members, and a plan for board training. If you do not use the information to make improvements, the evaluation process probably is not worth the effort.

The board that should be most open to individual evaluation is the one without term limits. Board members tend to get re-elected over and over even when their individual performance is commonly viewed as poor. But people who become friends are reluctant to be hard on one another — especially if the one with poor performance is also a major donor. Sometimes a board decides it is too big and tries to move a few inactive members into retirement through the announcement of an evaluation process. This may or may not be a good way to rid the board of deadwood.

Do many boards do individual evaluation? Not enough. And fewer do it well. So why should you undertake this somewhat sensitive step in building a good board? Because you are reading a book like this, we know you want your organization to have the best board possible. No individual or organization develops excellence without setting standards and submitting to some measure of accountability. Depending on where you are in your journey toward a five-star board, this exercise in board development should be considered.

We temper this recommendation with a word of caution. No board development activity, including self-evaluation, should create divisiveness, mistrust, or anger toward some. For this reason, it is important to initiate self-evaluation with the board's strong consensus that it is important to the long-term strength of the organization. Then the process must be developed with great sensitivity and fairness.

SUGGESTED ACTION STEPS

1. Ask board members who have served on boards that did individual evaluation to comment on their experiences.

2. Ask the board whether someone on the board should be asked to gather information on board member evaluation.

3. Ask the board development committee to draft a proposal for board member evaluation and bring it to the board for discussion.

Part IV

Board and Committee Meetings

How can we improve our meetings?

*"We get so bogged down in administrative matters that
we never do tackle the important things."*

Nonprofit board members frequently voice this complaint about the
way their boards function during meetings. Why do they have such a
penchant for doing staff work? Why can't they get down to the important
business of governance? Because it is hard work to express consensus on
values that reflect ends policies and to give the chief executive clear
parameters within which to work. But that skirts the question a bit on how
to improve board meetings.

Good governance requires several types of meetings: business meetings
of the full board, committee meetings, and ad hoc meetings. It also requires
opportunities for the board to meet informally at social gatherings. Most
board members we know rate their satisfaction more by their experience in
meetings than by their feelings about the mission or programs of an
organization. Part of joining a board is the expectation of making a
meaningful contribution and of having productive, enjoyable interaction

with peers. Beyond doing the homework for a meeting, serving on a board is about relationships. We suggest you consider each type of meeting and develop useful guidelines that work for your board.

FULL BOARD MEETINGS

Preparing for and conducting good meetings is an art form. Isn't it rewarding to serve on a board when you feel valued as a member and the group accomplishes so much in a few hours? Part of board excellence is searching continually for ways to improve meetings. It is our experience that board members who become disillusioned about their service do so most often because of poor board meetings. Everyone likes a meeting where there is good preparation, open discussion, clear consensus, and quick follow-up. Leadership usually makes these things happen, but each board member should feel accountable for helping make meetings effective. Here are 10 suggestions.

1. Great meetings build on prior basics.

It should go without saying that an organization needs a clear mission statement and organizational goals, committed board members with defined roles, and good communication between the board chair and the chief executive. Board meetings have limited potential without these basics.

2. Plan meetings well in advance.

The board's calendar is planned one year ahead, and the best possible meeting location is reserved. The board chair and the chief executive meet to set the agenda. Committee chairs are asked whether their committees will require board action on any recommendations or will simply provide informational reports. Time is allowed for presentation of materials and reports distributed in advance of the meeting.

3. Provide a positive environment.

Make the board feel important by providing the best physical environment possible for board and committee meetings. Pay attention to the basics: good lighting and ventilation, comfortable seats in a good arrangement. We think rented space in a nice retreat setting is worth the investment. Limit distractions as much as possible.

4. Put logistical details in place.

The details count: Advance written directions to the site, help with transportation needs, the right audiovisual equipment, refreshments available throughout the meeting, name cards on the table and name tags that are easily read at a distance, good seating arrangement allowing for board members and the chief executive to see one another around the table and other staff at a side table. There are a hundred details that staff need to coordinate to make the meeting memorable.

5. Manage the meeting effectively.

A strong presiding board chair is absolutely essential to an effective meeting. When the meeting is managed with a firm yet respectful hand, the participants will feel their time has been well spent and they have made a real contribution.

6. Follow the agenda.

A good meeting begins and ends on time. It follows the written agenda, although the board chair asks for changes to the agenda before the meeting begins. A distinction is made between items being presented to the board for information only and items requiring discussion and a vote. It is important, too, to allow time on the agenda for recognition of board and staff members for their efforts on behalf of the organization. A good day-long agenda, we find, goes something like this:

- Chair's comments
- Approval of agenda
- Approval of previous minutes
- Financial report
- Chief executive's report
- Committee meetings
- Committee reports and action
- Other business
- Executive session without staff present

Lunch is a good time to have an outside speaker, board training, or informal interaction with staff and constituents. Notice we do not advise a string of staff oral reports. Instead, send out two-page written reports in advance, and summarize them as part of the chief executive's report.

7. Allow ample time for discussion.

Board members agree on predetermined time limits for some discussion items, and time is provided for informal, "out-of-meeting" discussion. When the board is deliberating critical policies, it is a good idea to hold the discussion at one meeting and then take action at the next. Time should be set aside for board members to ask questions about the written staff reports mailed in advance.

8. Streamline the meeting with sound preparation.

The chief executive and staff should mail reports two weeks in advance of the board meeting. They should also anticipate other materials that might be needed. Past minutes, bylaws, the audit, the list of property owned, and other items can be kept in a looseleaf board reference book for use during meetings. Other handouts might have draft language for complicated resolutions or the pros and cons of a proposed policy. All committee chairs should be asked what they might want prepared for their meetings.

9. Hold an executive session without staff.

Some board members make mountains out of molehills when they do not have a chance to voice their concerns. Often these concerns have to do with staff actions. We think all boards deserve a regular opportunity to speak frankly without staff or guests present. The best way to defuse misunderstandings or head off a problem before it becomes serious is to provide a routine time for the board to meet alone. Usually an executive session works best as the last agenda item. These sessions may last only five or ten minutes, but if an hour is necessary, it should be allowed. Some boards meet first with their chief executive, then alone. Staff should not feel threatened. Executive sessions are just one way to build a positive, productive board.

10. Start follow up immediately after the meeting.

Staff are understandably tired and anxious to get back to work after most board meetings. But good meetings include immediate follow-up: thank-you letters, minutes, assignment of policy decisions, staff briefings, a phone debriefing between the board chair and the chief executive. The chief executive gains credibility when he or she sends a memo to the board one week after a meeting to explain how the staff is implementing recent board decisions. Often, timing is everything.

COMMITTEE MEETINGS

Some smaller boards function without standing committees, but most boards choose to have a few. Common ones are the executive committee, board development committee, audit committee, finance committee, and program committee. Many boards create special committees or task forces to function for specific times on more focused issues. A key principle to remember is that board committees are created to help the board do its work, not to oversee staff work (see Chapter 17 for more about committees).

Most of a committee's work is done in meetings. Like board meetings, committee meetings should be carefully planned and executed. Some of the principles of good board meetings apply, of course, but committee meetings also have unique features. We offer these suggestions:

1. Define each committee's purpose and responsibilities in the standing policies of the board.

These written policies should cover the committee's job description, who appoints the chair, chair's term limit, inclusion of nonboard members as committee members, and staff assistance.

2. Appoint a chair who is willing and able to manage the committee.

Chairing a committee takes time and requires group process skills, which not all board members possess. Obviously, it helps if the chair has expertise in the subject area.

3. Assign a staff member as a resource.

This staff liaison, designated by the chief executive, works with the committee chair on such tasks as developing materials, recording committee actions, and sending out notices on behalf of the chair. The chief executive should always be the staff representative to the executive committee and possibly to the board development committee.

4. The chair should develop the agenda with suggestions from others.

The board chair, committee members, and the chief executive or staff liaison may be consulted, along with the standing policies manual sections that relate to the committee. Committee meetings should be devoted to policy review and recommendations as well as to strategic thinking about the organization's future, in the context of the committee's responsibility.

5. Consider a committee reference book for use during meetings.

The staff could maintain a looseleaf notebook that is available during committee meetings along with the board reference book described above. Committee members can refer to the notebook for information related to the committee's role.

6. Follow up promptly on committee meetings.

Resolutions to be forwarded to the board should be approved in writing. After the meeting, the chair should communicate immediately with the chief executive and board chair regarding committee items for the next board agenda. (This could literally happen within the hour.) Send minutes to committee members for approval and to board members as background for upcoming agenda items.

Some committees have unique issues that may affect their meetings. The finance committee, for example, must resist getting so deeply into the details that it loses track of its broader role: to help the board adopt sound parameters guiding executive actions in the finance area. This committee could invite outside experts to talk about such topics as investment options or new insurance products. The board development (or nominating) committee has much advance work to do in identifying and checking out prospective board members before committee discussion. When this committee is discussing board structure and process, the board chair and chief executive should be invited to attend (they are usually *ex officio* members of all committees).

AD HOC MEETINGS

How often have you gone to lunch or met briefly for coffee with a staff member or fellow board member to discuss an organizational matter? Sometimes the meeting is just a phone call. These informal meetings are quite frequent and another aspect of governance. Here are some tips for making them productive:

- Make the purpose of the meeting clear to all participants.
- Be sure one person has all the information the group needs.
- Conversations usually go better when someone assumes the lead role.
- Assign a participant to follow up on the areas of conclusion.
- Document the meeting in written form, if appropriate.
- Inform others who need to know the results of the meeting.

Informal meetings between the board chair and the chief executive, or a few members of a committee prior to the full committee meeting, are necessary to keep things on track. But avoid the situation in which the board gets used to trusting a few people to do what should be official business. Then the full board is left uninformed and out of touch, and matters that need formal board approval are left out of the record. There are legal as well as functional reasons to keep ad hoc meetings in proper perspective.

SOCIAL GATHERINGS

You may wonder why we include social gatherings in our chapter about meetings. We think it is unfortunate that some boards never meet socially except at coffee breaks. Good board policies flow from mutual respect, trust, and loyalty among board members and between board members and staff. A board builds these qualities best through interaction outside the board room.

Time spent in a relaxed setting — at the home of the chief executive or a board member, on the tennis court or golf course, at a picnic — are invaluable for building good working relationships. Usually a few board members are good at helping the group bond through these informal times. Take advantage of their gifts of hospitality, humor, or creative ideas for group interaction. Involve families as much as possible, for they provide the support that enables board members to devote occasional weekends and evenings to board service.

We strongly urge an annual retreat for all board members. A retreat is a productive time for long-term thinking, working on a better mission statement, evaluating how the board is functioning, getting training in an area critical to board success, or just getting to know a new chief executive. But it is also a social time. Dress casually and comfortably. Enjoy each other's company, take walks, talk informally about the future and how the organization will deal with it. There is nothing quite like it.

Attention to the details of meetings is well worth the effort. Meetings should really be memorable "events." They are the primary process that allows an organization to define itself, its goals, and the policies that will ensure its success. Don't ignore this important element of good governance.

SUGGESTED ACTION STEPS

1. Survey board members to find out how meetings could be improved. Provide a summary of the results and show that you heard the feedback by adopting changes.

2. Develop criteria for selecting the board and committee chairs that include proven ability to plan and preside at meetings.

3. Ask around (including your board members who serve on other boards as well as chief executives and other board members known to your group) to learn which boards conduct good meetings. Borrow their practices if they fit with your organization's structure and traditions.

4. Be sure staff are assigned to each committee and know their boundaries in working with committee chairs.

32

How often and where should a board meet?

"We meet every month, but half the time we accomplish little."

A board should meet only as many times as are required to fulfill its role, and it should hold meetings wherever the setting is most conducive to quality board work. These are deceptively simple answers, because it is amazing how often boards do otherwise. For example, an organization may have adopted bylaws years ago, when it had no professional staff, that said the board would meet monthly. This practice continues long beyond its usefulness, and you can guess what happens. Attendance drops, agendas are filled with management issues rather than governance issues, the staff spends too much time in preparation, and it is difficult to recruit new board members who can meet that often. Or a board meets in the small conference room at the organization's headquarters. The cramped setting is not conducive to large-group work, and board members have a hard time staying focused. When asked why the board has never had a change of scenery, the board chair says, "We've *always* met in the small conference room."

According to a 1997 survey by BoardSource (formerly the National Center for Nonprofit Boards), the median number of meetings among nonprofits is seven per year. Most organizations require an annual meeting at which board members and officers are elected. A few small organizations with a limited focus may find that one day a year is enough to keep on track. On the other extreme, it may be necessary to meet monthly in the first phase of organizational life, then reduce the frequency to whatever is appropriate for that phase of the organization's life cycle.

For many national or international organizations of whatever size, two meetings per year usually work well. One meeting lasts an evening and a full day, and the other is a two-evening, three-day retreat. The board can meet by conference call as necessary and depend on the executive committee to meet and act on its behalf if there is an urgent requirement. Many experienced board members agree that an annual retreat, where issues have time to be discussed informally at meals and breaks, is a more productive investment of time than an equal number of hours spread over two or three different meetings. Technology can improve communications and reduce the number of live meetings necessary to get the same amount of work done. Some meetings today can be private chat rooms or listservs that allow discussion and informal consensus in advance of the official meeting.

Organizations that are truly investing thought and energy in good governance are imaginative about where they meet. Think of a board meeting as a "happening" with the following activity modules:

- Informal time for fellowship
- Learning about the organization, including firsthand observation
- Committee meetings
- Governance training, including board self-assessment
- Meeting staff, clients, and vendors
- Learning about the organization's environment, including other organizations, the community, and the local economy
- Business session for formal decisions

- Brainstorming session to think about the future

- Executive session

These modules offer possibilities for different settings, which could vary according to the purpose of the event. It is important to use time wisely, but a 20-minute van ride to another site offers an opportunity for board members to get better acquainted with one another and with staff. For national and international boards, the site could rotate to reduce the long trips some board members have to make and to give the board different experiences related to the organization's programs.

Here are some inventive ideas for places to hold board meetings:

- A city hall hearing room for a briefing on demographic and economic trends

- A tour of the organization's facility with several "briefing stops" along the way

- A visit to a program site where the organization is working

- A retreat center in tranquil surroundings conducive to strategic thinking

- A place to observe staff serving the primary beneficiaries of the organization

- A high-tech conference room at a local business

- A bus tour of sites being served by the organization, with business conducted on the bus

The objective is to choose a setting that helps make the meeting memorable. Even a day in the same conference room can include guest speakers, staff presentations, a reception for new staff, a video link with people at another site, and bulletin boards with special displays. Meeting planners are often so focused on the business agenda and the board book preparation that special features are shortchanged.

SUGGESTED ACTION STEPS

1. Ask each board member to write down how many meetings per year seem ideal for the organization at this stage in its life cycle. Average the number and discuss the results.

2. Ask whether the board would like one retreat (with at least one overnight) instead of one regular meeting. You may be surprised, and board members may be willing to pay for it.

3. Beginning with the list above, ask the board to brainstorm for 10 minutes on future settings for board meetings.

33

Who should attend board meetings, and what are their roles?

*"Our meetings look more like conventions
than board meetings."*

Board meetings fulfill the governance role of a nonprofit organization. The simple answer to this question is to invite as many people as will improve the organization's governance and mission. Each meeting might be different, and old traditions may no longer be relevant. The assumption that board members and the chief executive are the only participants may not be the best assumption. Here is a list of possible participants and their roles.

- *Board members.* Every board member should make it a priority to attend every meeting.

- *Chief executive.* The board chair and the chief executive should sit next to one another during business sessions, working as a team. This principle makes sense, but the chief executive should be a nonvoting *ex officio* member.

- *Senior staff.* Those who report to the chief executive and serve as staff aides to committees should be invited to most board meeting sessions. They should sit apart from the board, listen and learn, and be ready to provide information when called upon by the chief executive (who cannot, after all, be expected to know every detail of the operation). Breaks and meals allow for personal interaction between board and staff. Sometimes a senior staff member makes a presentation; for example, the chief financial officer may make the financial report and brief the board on the budget.

- *Other staff.* Usually other staff are invited only for special purposes. For example, three people who conducted a study may report their conclusions directly to the board, or staff members are invited to join the board for a break or lunch. It is important that board members and staff meet, but they can do so at award banquets, receptions, or during board tours of the facilities.

- *Auditor.* A representative of the firm that performed the external audit is often invited for a brief report to the board. This may not be necessary every year, but there is nothing like hearing from the auditor that the finances are being managed well and the organization is solvent.

- *Board trainer/mentor.* Some boards invite an outside person — a former board member or a consultant — to monitor their meetings and give feedback on how they can improve. Usually, this person sits apart from the board table, observes, and takes five minutes at the end to make helpful comments. The board trainer/mentor often meets with the chair and chief executive alone to provide additional recommendations for their roles.

- *Emeritus board members.* Some boards grant this honorary title to a few distinguished former board members. Other boards create an alumni council for all board members who served more than a specified number of years. Through this mechanism, quality people stay committed to the organization after they leave the board. If the board allows emeritus members to participate in discussions but not vote, they should be seated at the table. If not, a special table to the side of the room should be provided.

- *Board members' spouses.* Spouses may be invited at least to the annual retreat or to another meeting. The chair may determine that they may sit in on part of the meeting, or invite them for the opening segment, the reception, and the meal and then offer special activities outside the boardroom. For some board members to give their best to the organization, a supportive spouse is essential.

- *Guest presenter.* An attorney, an architect, a consultant who has just evaluated the organization's fund-raising operation, or a similar outside expert may be invited for a specific time slot in the agenda. He or she is introduced, gives a short presentation, responds to questions, and then is thanked and excused from the meeting. To save time, these presentations often take place over lunch.

- *Prospective board members.* Frequently, a top candidate for board membership is invited to observe a board meeting before making a final decision. This can be an informative step both for the board and for the candidate.

- *Prospective major donor.* Before agreeing to make a major contribution, it is reasonable for a donor to ask to sit in on a board meeting. If you acquiesce, be prepared and understand the inherent risk. How effectively you run your meeting can either convince the donor to partner with you or can turn him or her away with disappointment.

- *Primary beneficiaries.* Perhaps there are people your organization serves who would be honored to tell their stories to the board. This is a win-win idea because the board is always gratified to see the results of the organization's efforts. These participants would be scheduled for a specific time — perhaps over lunch, allowing for personal interaction.

When deciding who should attend, remember that a board meeting should not be a convention. Board members should be expected to attend a reasonable number of additional events, so some activities — such as a visit with beneficiaries or a guest speaker — could be scheduled at other times.

Before leaving this topic, we recommend having two types of executive sessions at the end of every board meeting: one with just the chief executive present and one with volunteer board members only. It is important for board members and the chief executive to have time alone with each other to express concerns or ask questions that are not easily handled with others in the room. Then the volunteer board members should meet alone to bring up issues that would not be discussed with the chief executive present.

The board may decide who attends board meetings, with one significant exception. Some states have open meeting laws — sometimes called sunshine laws — that apply to organizations receiving government funding. These laws vary from state to state, but the principle is to promote public accountability and ensure that important decisions relating to the use of taxpayer dollars are known. These laws can build public trust. They also can frustrate board members when people with a particular ax to grind show up and demand they be heard.

SUGGESTED ACTION STEPS

1. Ask each board member, allowing confidential responses, whether he or she feels comfortable with the people who usually attend meetings.

2. Take five minutes to brainstorm who the board would like to include on its agenda at the next few meetings.

3. Establish a rule that only board members sit at the board table and be permitted to speak without being asked.

34

How should staff participate in board and committee meetings?

"At my first board meeting, I remember not being able to distinguish board members from senior staff."

Staff have an important role in board meetings but, except for the chief executive, they fulfill this role primarily before the board arrives for the meeting. The patterns vary considerably among the boards we know, but some principles work well in most instances. (Be sure to review Chapter 46 for additional information on staff contributions to governance.)

THE CHIEF EXECUTIVE

In addition to working closely with the board chair on substantive preparation for board meetings, the chief executive has a critical role once the meeting begins. Especially in larger organizations, it is common for the chief executive — but no other staff — to serve ex officio as a board member. The challenge is for the chief executive to help the board *be* the board (recall that a properly oriented board does not compete with the chief executive for leadership) by not giving too much or too little of his or her own opinion. The servant-leadership model is the proper relationship. Here are some key points about the chief executive's role:

- Although we don't want to be too strict on this point, we like the protocol of board members referring all questions to the chief executive, who can then choose to answer them or to call on staff colleagues in the room.

- Helping the board chair manage the meeting is an important way for the chief executive to help meetings stay focused and productive. By sitting next to the board chair, the chief executive can make quiet suggestions or point out details on the documents being reviewed.

- We think it is smart for chief executives to suggest the practice of routinely holding executive sessions at the end of every business meeting. A chief executive should always let the board know he or she trusts them and wants them to function as openly and candidly as they choose. Some boards have two sessions: first with the chief executive and no one else, then without the chief executive.

- The chief executive can take the initiative to add a special spark to meetings: A reception at his or her home, a gift of appreciation, special help with travel to and from the airport. The chief executive is in the most advantageous position to help board members feel positive about their meetings.

SENIOR STAFF

There is a natural motivation for staff to "show their stuff" to the board. Some wisely know that board members want to function independently and not depend on staff. And it is not the staff's role to dictate what they should do. It is difficult for competent staff, who know so much more than their board members on most issues, to sit back and watch at board meetings. But sit back and watch is what we think most staff, except for the chief executive, should be prepared to do. We like boards who allow senior staff to attend board meetings because it is a great education for staff and builds better communication and trust. Here are some key points for senior staff to know:

- Prepare excellent written reports for your areas of responsibility and send them to board members in advance of meetings. These reports should be approved by the chief executive and be thorough yet concise, making comparisons, pointing out the major options, and giving recom-mendations and the basis for them.

- At the board meeting, be content to wait for board members to ask questions. There is seldom need for oral reports from staff.

- Help the chief executive put special touches on board meetings. Pick board members up at the airport. Give them a behind-the-scenes look at the organization. Offer to gather information they express interest in and mail it to them later.

- For committee meetings, senior staff usually function more openly. Just as the chief executive wants to help the board become stronger in its role, so other staff should try to guide and support committees.

Without compromising basic issues of integrity, senior staff need to demonstrate their support of the chief executive and the management team and reflect loyalty to the organization and its mission. Even though they may not speak much during a board meeting, board members pick up signals about the status of the organization as they watch staff.

BOARD SECRETARY

It is advisable to have a staff member who takes care of board communications, arranges travel, drafts board minutes, makes sure the room is set up properly, and handles other important logistics. This person is often an assistant to the chief executive. Sometimes he or she has longer tenure than most staff and board members and becomes an informal board historian. This staff member should be formally elected as an assistant secretary of the board so routine documents required by banks and insurance companies can have an official signature. He or she, or the chief financial officer, is also elected as an assistant treasurer for similar reasons.

Staff are necessary, but not sufficient, for excellence in organizational governance. We commend the bright, committed people who choose a career in the nonprofit sector. And we firmly believe that as they help their boards become stronger, they will discover new freedom in exercising their own judgment and skills in their management roles.

SUGGESTED ACTION STEPS

1. Ask board members what they think staff could do to improve committee meetings.

2. Consider how the chief executive's role as it relates to board meetings can improve the organization even more.

3. Invite staff to brainstorm how they could improve the next board meeting.

35

What are the different ways boards make decisions?

"We get all tied up in Robert's Rules of Order, and it slows us down."

You might be surprised at the range of perspectives on how a board comes to conclusions. Some use informal consensus, most require a simple majority (or a "super" majority on important items), and still others require unanimity on all decisions. A guiding principle is that when the board is making a decision, the process should be fair, open, and recorded. Many other decisions — such as meeting locations, agendas, advance materials, and board reports — are made legitimately for the board by the board chair or the chief executive.

A few boards may follow Robert's Rules of Order, but frankly, a less rigid approach to the governance process is best. At a minimum, it's a good idea to spell out voting requirements in your bylaws. Good dialogue prior to decisions is the goal. For complex topics, sometimes the chair will need to adjourn a business meeting temporarily, let someone else guide open discussion, and then reconvene the business meeting.

Here are the major ways boards make decisions:

- *Simple majority vote.* This is the classic method. The chair either asks for a voice vote, declaring his sense of the majority subject to objection, or asks for a show of hands. We all know a veteran (and impatient) chair who will rattle off, "All in favor say aye; all opposed no; the ayes have it; the motion is passed" — without even looking up from his notes. Most board votes are unanimous, but not necessarily because they are rubber-stamp actions. Those quick, unanimous votes can also reflect legitimate agreement after much good discussion of the options.

- *Super-majority vote.* Some decisions — amending the bylaws, firing the chief executive, or approving real estate transactions, for example — require more than a simple majority. Sometimes the preference is for two-thirds, sometimes for three-fourths. The bylaws might outline other important decisions that should require a super-majority.

  An important related question is the definition of a quorum. A quorum requirement of only one-third of the board members, followed by a simple majority, allows for a very few to make decisions. At the opposite end of the spectrum, a two-thirds quorum might be required for important business like hiring or firing a chief executive.

- *Consensus.* This word has several meanings, so each board must be sure everyone agrees on its use. A chair might listen to discussion and say, "I believe we have consensus. Let the minutes show the board approves." While expedient, this more casual approach has its drawbacks. Did the chair read the sense of the board accurately? Or did many people who were thinking against an idea not voice their concerns at that point? For final action, a voice or hand vote is preferable.

  Consensus can have a positive use as a condition for taking a vote. In this case, the chair wants everyone to have a fair opportunity to be heard. After what he or she thinks has been adequate discussion, the chair might ask, "Is there consensus [total agreement] that it's time to vote?" That is a signal for those who have been holding back to have their say.

- *Unanimity only.* Some boards, especially some in particular religious traditions, believe it is important to reach total unanimity before any board action is final. The spirit of this approach is admirable, but it rarely works well. First, some would argue that the whole reason for having a group of 9, 15, or 21 board members is to bring a diversity of views to the table. The practice of required unanimity tends to silence those who would otherwise take a different view unless they think it is of critical importance. Others may feel unspoken pressure to go along with the perceived majority at the time of voting, only to feel like a hypocrite later. It is possible for a board to enjoy great unity while encouraging board members to speak and vote their true conscience. In other words, a board can have unity without unanimity on all votes.

A board having this tradition, but not sure of its value at this point, might consider process rules that require consensus (meaning unanimity) of the board before moving to a vote. Or it could require a majority vote on routine matters, a super-majority on some issues, and unanimity on a few others.

OPEN VOTING VS. SECRET BALLOT

In most cases, open voting is preferable for nonprofit boards. Votes should be taken in the presence of staff or others who happen to be at the meeting. Sometimes a board might go into executive session for good reasons, but the board members still see who votes how. This approach creates trust over the long run.

An exception is the interesting practice of choosing board officers by secret ballot. In the touchy situation of a board voting to terminate one of its members, the person at issue would usually be asked to step out of the room, but even then the chair might wisely decide on a written secret ballot.

RECORDING DECISIONS

It isn't necessary to take the space in board minutes to record who made a motion and who seconded it, and then who amended the same motion. Usually, just "MSC: Lou Leader be elected chair for one term" is sufficient. On first use, the longer "Moved, seconded, and carried (MSC)" could explain this shorthand. Some boards do roll call votes, and the minutes show who voted and how. In other situations, a chair will declare the results of the vote and a board member will request "the minutes record that I voted against."

SUGGESTED ACTION STEPS

1. Just after a vote, have the chair announce, "We're going to take 15 minutes to review how the board makes its decisions so I'm confident that we're doing it according to the board's wishes."

2. Ask your legal advisor to suggest how the bylaws could reflect good decision-making practices that others use.

3. Put the decision-making issue on the agenda of your board development committee.

36

How can technology improve board and committee meetings?

"Technology could help us so much, but many board members are afraid of it."

Technology is changing the way most nonprofits do business. Will it also change the way boards conduct their business? Yes and no. Technology has great potential for streamlining the board's work. But state law governs the way nonprofit organizations make policy, and states are slow to update their statutes. Let's look at each area in which technology might be applied.

LIVE MEETINGS

Most boards will choose to conduct their meetings in person for the forseeable future. People join boards because they like group dynamics. Dialogue — in which one can notice nonverbal cues and read the tone of another's remarks — is essential for group decision making. Besides, any change in an average board of 19 will meet with some resistance.

Yet who can deny technology has improved live meetings? Listening to PowerPoint presentations, reviewing the organization's Web site, learning from a video, and taking minutes on a laptop computer are all common features of board meetings. A few organizations with large boards have found various forms of group decision-making software useful even during a live meeting. A few others "meet" via videoconference, which can be expensive and provide little benefit other than saving some board members travel time and expense.

Technology can be most useful between live meetings and in committee meetings. Since committees are simply preparing recommendations for board action, few state laws prevent the use of chat rooms and e-lists for discussion and decision making on routine issues.

TELEPHONE CONFERENCE CALLS

Conference calls are useful for boards and committees whose members know one another well and agree that the quality of decision making won't be compromised significantly. Again, committees can make better use of this technology than full boards. Conference calls take better planning, good advance materials, a strong chair, and an agreed-upon protocol to make it a smooth experience. Conference calls may reduce the number of board meetings; a board that used to meet four times a year could meet twice with conference calls in between. The cost is becoming more affordable, and it is easy to arrange a toll-free number so board members calling in can be connected at the predetermined time.

CONSENT MINUTES

Many nonprofit organizations allow formal board action without meeting, although they may use this method infrequently. Consent minutes are useful for timely, noncontroversial decisions when it is impossible to call an actual meeting or rally a quorum for a conference call. An e-mail or fax to all board members, requesting a written or electronic signature in return, is the quickest method. A week or two in advance, you could encourage dialogue through an e-list or a chat room discussion on the organization's Web site so board members feel prepared for decision making by consent minutes. Consent minutes require unanimity, so if even one board member opposes a proposal, this method will not work.

OTHER TECHNOLOGY ADVANCES

How else could board meetings be improved through technology? Here are some ideas:

- Create a Web site for the board, accessible to board members and senior staff by password. Use it for such things as orienting new board members, archiving minutes, or posting discussion papers for the next board meeting.

- Try a regular chat room where interested board members can exchange views on complex issues that will be on a future board meeting agenda. If your state statute and your bylaws allow it, you can use this technology to actually come to a formal board decision.

- E-lists help the board chair or chief executive test ideas and options several weeks in advance of a meeting. They also contribute to early dialogue and lead to improved, shorter live discussion at the meeting.

- Web sites and e-mail can link the board with its constituencies, an important function for the board. Surveys and feedback on proposed actions could improve the quality of board decisions.

Emerging technologies are useful assets for governance, but experience shows that some cautions are in order.

- Technology is not foolproof. Just when you want to depend on it, it may not work.

- Not everyone is skilled at using the Internet. Be prepared to train board members.

- Some advanced applications are expensive and require staff support.

- Using technology still turns off some board members.
- Words on the computer screen — in e-mail or chat rooms — often are interpreted differently than the spoken word.
- Privacy is important on some issues; be wary of hackers.

In the end, the quality of the decision is what matters most. Saving time in order to reach poor decisions may not be worth it.

On the other side of the coin, delaying the application of proven, well-known technologies is another caution. Increasingly, savvy board members will expect their organizations to be up to speed. Technology can be a motivator, it can save time and expense, and it can build a complete record of board discussion. Stay tuned: Answers to this chapter's question will change every year.

SUGGESTED ACTION STEPS

1. Try multiple technologies with one of your committees. Send an e-mail directing them to your Web site for a proposal. Invite committee members to make their comments in a chat-room format for two weeks, and then schedule a telephone conference to reach consensus.

2. Assign interested board members and staff to a task force that meets with experts and reports to the board on potential uses of new technologies.

Part V

Board-Staff Relations

37

What is the board's role in human resource matters?

"We get too involved because we know that staff salaries make up 80 percent of the budget."

Boards are involved in human resource matters with respect to the chief executive, but generally not with respect to other staff. There are different views on this subject, and some boards do get more involved with other human resource decisions. Think of the board's role as having five consecutive steps: adopting board policies, modeling those policies with the chief executive, delegating human resource decisions to the chief executive, deciding budget issues relating to staff, and monitoring staff.

I. Adopt board policies.

The board sets the context for human resource issues by adopting general policies that fit the organization at this point in its history. These policies, usually described succinctly in the standing policies manual, can address some of the following issues:

- To what extent should the organization plan its services to tap as much volunteer staff as possible? Should volunteers' expenses be reimbursed?

- Does the board want to establish staff compensation levels that are less than, equal to, or more than the average for similar organizations? Comparison data are fairly easy to obtain.

- To be competitive and reduce employees' taxes, to what extent does the organization want to be known for offering good benefits? Specifically, how much of the cost should the organization bear for health, dental, vision, and life insurance? Should there be a pension plan, and what should the employee contribution be? Should staff receive coupons for using public transportation? How about free parking?

- Should there be an emphasis on promoting from within?

- Does the board endorse performance-based compensation?

- Should human resource policies encourage long-term employment, or should the board assume a three- to four-year tenure?

2. Model the policies with the chief executive.

How the board recruits, compensates, evaluates, and terminates its one agent — the chief executive — will speak volumes to staff who are involved in human resource matters with other staff. Obviously, the board should reflect its general policies in how it deals with the chief executive.

3. Delegate all other human resource decisions to the chief executive.

Disagreement may surface here. Because salaries are such a big part of the budget, many boards like to be the ultimate authority in hiring and compensating at least the senior staff members. We don't recommend this practice. By becoming involved to this degree, the board risks marginalizing the chief executive's authority and expectations of staff loyalty and trust. Besides, the board is far too removed from day-to-day operations to be able to make choices, set salary levels, and evaluate staff they see just a few times a year. Successful delegation of this authority to the chief executive requires, however, that the board do a good job of articulating its philosophy of staffing.

4. Decide budget issues relating to staff.

The budget is another tool the board can use to influence human resource matters. The board can decide what percentage increase the new budget should include for staff salaries, but the chief executive is in the best position to determine how to allocate that amount among across-the-board increases, merit increases, or adjustments to keep up with the market. Within the budget, the board could also specify limits on items such as health insurance or pension plan contributions.

5. Monitor staffing.

As in all areas where the board sets policy, it should define how it wants to monitor those policies. The board should ask for reports on matters such as staffing levels, salaries, evaluation procedures, and management of incentive pay. If the board sees things that most board members feel are damaging to the organization, it should revise its policies and expect the chief executive to make corresponding changes. Obviously, a good chief executive checks informally with board members before making any major decisions that are likely to trouble the staff.

A board can adjust its role in human resource matters depending on the organization's needs. For example, perhaps the chief executive wants the finance committee to interview the top three candidates for the chief financial officer. The committee can provide useful feedback, but the decision belongs to the chief executive, to whom the chief financial officer would report.

The staff should feel good if the board is clear on general policies, treats the chief executive fairly, expects all human resource decisions to comply with the law, raises sufficient funds for equitable salaries, and then lets the chief executive manage the staff needed to accomplish the organization's mission. When boards delve more deeply into the specifics of how staff are hired, trained, compensated, evaluated, or terminated, both the staff and the board ultimately suffer.

SUGGESTED ACTION STEPS

1. Ask the board to review the items in step 1 above. Should the board clarify its philosophy on some of those items?

2. If the board seems too involved in selecting staff or setting salaries, ask a neutral consultant to interview staff and board members to assess the impact of the board's role and make suggestions.

38

Should staff serve on the board?

"Because three staff sit on our board, we depend on them pretty much to explain the various issues and help us make the decisions."

As the backbone of nonprofit organizations, boards are accountable for stewardship of the public's investment in their charitable mission. For-profit corporations routinely put paid executives on their boards. Nonprofits need to pursue good business practices, but they are not pursuing profits. They are changing lives and providing services. In exchange, they receive contributions and tax benefits. Accountability to our major moral owners suggests a separation of power, a set of checks and balances that comes from distinguishing the role of the board from that of the staff.

In general, the only staff member who might be justified to sit on a board is the chief executive. Some advocate voting rights for the chief executive to reflect a true peer relationship while working with the board. Others believe the chief executive should be a nonvoting board member because of the inevitable conflicts of interest.

Some surveys find that less than two percent of those who serve on the boards of charitable organizations receive compensation for their service. (An organization may compensate a board member for duties other than serving as a board member.) A Canadian court found that to be a paid staff member and then fill the role of a volunteer board member of the same organization is, on the face of it, a conflict of interest.

In our opinion, the ideal model is a volunteer board of competent and committed people setting policy and overseeing the work of staff. As a board, they have one agent to implement policy: the chief executive. In many of the organizations with which we are familiar, however, the chief executive is also a full voting member of the board. The reasons for this practice include:

- The chief executive was a founder who incorporated the organization and helped recruit the first board members.

- The chief executive is, by virtue of age and experience, a true peer among board members and wants to be treated as such.

- A new chief executive insists on board membership as a condition of employment.

Frankly, these are not strong arguments. A founding chief executive should be building a board that can fill the board role independently. A chief executive who does a good job should never feel insecure or looked down upon by board peers just because he or she does not sit on the board.

Consider that board members are expected to vote their consciences on every action. The chief executive's job is to support the board by implementing its decisions. He or she needs to maintain the confidence and trust of the entire board, building relationships that promote effective interaction. Why put the chief executive in the position of ever having to vote against any board members?

We like the "without vote" clause in the bylaws for chief executives who are given a board seat. Membership on the board should be ex officio — by virtue of position — not elected. Periodically voting whether or not the chief executive should be a board member is not the best way to signal approval or disapproval of job performance.

Even without a vote on the board, most chief executives have far more influence over board decisions than they may realize. Every chief executive should be seated next to the chair during all business meetings (except executive sessions). He or she should have the right to speak as a board member. In fact, most questions during debate are directed to the chief executive. When handled wisely, this power far exceeds most board members' abilities to influence board policy.

How does a no-vote policy for staff affect board members? It encourages them to take their jobs more seriously and prevents automatic deferral to the views of staff, who have greater programmatic experience. They view their chair as the key leader. They cannot depend on staff to fill both board and staff roles. They learn more easily the distinction between board work and staff work.

We should add our strong feeling that no paid staff other than the chief executive should be members of the board. In addition to the concerns we have already shared, here's another: Board membership for some staff but not others creates divisions. Why should some have authority over their peers in decisions about budget, salaries and benefits, and program priorities? The board can benefit from the staff's experience and perspectives without putting them on the board.

We do believe that senior staff should attend board meetings. We say more about this topic in Chapters 33 and 34.

SUGGESTED ACTION STEPS

1. Check the organization's bylaws for their clarity on the matter of board membership for staff. Discuss the pros and cons, and then make the bylaws clear.

2. To be certain that the board feels good about a situation in which a staff member has a vote, invite an impartial person to survey board members.

3. If you are the chief executive, make a list of the pros and cons of your own board membership, with or without vote, from your perspective. Talk with your chair about whether you should initiate change or clarify this matter with the board.

39

Should board members
be hired as staff?

*"John has been a committed board member for several years,
but I get the impression he'd like to be more hands-on
with the programs — possibly as a staff member."*

This situation often surprises boards that haven't thought about the possibility — but it does exist. One very fast-growing nonprofit organization, after about five years, had more than 15 former board members serving on the staff. Such a situation has problems worth exploring.

First, however, let's be clear on a simple point: There should be nothing wrong with an organization hiring someone who happens to sit on its board, as long as two principles are observed:

- The organization follows an open process that results in hiring the best candidate.

- No board member serves simultaneously on the staff except the chief executive.

The organization should guard against the following problematic practices:

- There is no open competition showing that the board member is the most qualified candidate.

- The board's behavior suggests that interested board members should be "promoted" to paid staff as an incentive to join the board.

- The chief executive holds out the possibility of well-paying jobs for board members as a way of controlling their behavior.

- The board member wants to remain on the board, once on the payroll.

This last problem is particularly challenging. Suppose a popular and contributing board member is hired, everyone sees the merits of the appointment, and he or she insists on remaining on the board. There are too many conflicts of interest for a board member other than the chief executive to serve on the board. Besides, a staff member who goes to a board meeting as a board member and then returns to staff meetings is bound to create morale problems with other staff. If your board does not have a policy on this matter (and most do not), consider developing a simple statement that puts the responsibility on the shoulders of each board member to resign if he or she is offered — or even wants to apply for — a staff position.

A stronger board policy might even be called for — for example, no board member may accept a paid position with the organization until he or she has been off the board for one year. A similar policy applies to members of Congress, who are not allowed to lobby their peers for one year after terminating their service.

What should an organization do if some board members already work as paid employees? Ideally the board chair should ask the board members to step down from one of the positions. At a minimum, the board chair and chief executive should draft guidelines that could prevent embarrassing situations in the future. Although the staff morale issue is hard to deal with in policies, these guidelines would help:

- Board members who are employees may not discuss board business with staff other than as required by the chief executive.

- These individuals must maintain confidentialities in both settings, as appropriate.

- These individuals must excuse themselves from any specific board discussion when they, the chair, the chief executive, or any two members of the board suggest that they be excused.

Two other dimensions to this issue remain. First, many nonprofit organizations have volunteers who carry significant responsibilities. It should not be a problem for board members to volunteer for one of these tasks. Second, it may be acceptable to retain a board member as a paid consultant for a short-term assignment following an open selection process.

SUGGESTED ACTION STEPS

1. If a board member other than the chief executive serves on the paid staff, consider asking a neutral consultant to interview board members and staff confidentially and report to the board for an honest discussion on this matter.

2. If no board members serve on the staff, consider adding a policy now that says the chief executive is the only board member who may also be a paid staff member.

40

What are the characteristics of the best nonprofit chief executives?

"He is really committed, but I don't think he has what it takes to be a chief executive."

Nine chief executives gathered for three days of dialogue about their leadership styles. One, a dynamic visionary, could get almost anyone to follow her. Another, from a military background, was a tough-minded, no-nonsense manager. One man was so quiet and gentle you wondered how he led his large organization. The "clown" of the group kept everyone laughing, and you wondered if this represented her normal style. The others were just as unique. We all were struck by the diversity of personality types who carried the chief executive label.

Almost all chief executives want to improve. They watch how their peers function and then compare their own styles and procedures. What makes that person so successful? Why is the other one not making it? What common characteristics make an effective leader?

Boards searching for chief executives ask similar questions. No one person can meet all the expectations a group of people may have, so a board must say what it believes are the essentials for leading the organization. When a board decides it must terminate one chief executive, the group often swings the pendulum far to the other side and hires someone with strengths in the areas of the former leader's weaknesses. Soon, a different set of constituents are unhappy; they miss the characteristics of the one who left.

The literature on leadership is plentiful, and research on what makes a good leader will probably continue forever. But there will never be one conclusive set of characteristics all boards should look for in a chief executive, for two simple reasons: Organizations need a different style of executive leadership at different stages of growth, and more than one leadership style could work in an organization at any given time. Having said this, we do find some common characteristics among successful chief executives. Here are some requirements that are almost universal in nonprofit organizations.

VISION BEARER

The chief executive must be skilled at articulating and promoting the vision and mission that guides the organization. The familiar proverb, "Without a vision, the people perish" applies to nonprofit organizations as well. People follow men and women who know where they are going. In start-up organizations, the chief executive is often the founder and keeper of the vision that attracts board members, volunteers, and donors. The vision creates excitement. Sustaining that initial excitement depends heavily on the chief executive. In a mature organization — one that has had, say, five or more chief executives — the chief executive must sometimes move slowly in changing the vision because so many are now aware of it and believe in it. But he or she must embrace the vision and find new ways for people to relate to it.

Without a compelling vision, a chief executive will have short tenure. If you are a chief executive without a vision that energizes your daily work, we urge you to focus on that issue. Either create one the board endorses, work with your board to define one, or consider moving on. That is blunt advice, but it underscores the importance we put on this characteristic of the best chief executives.

PERSUADER/MOTIVATOR

Do you know people who have an idea or a vision that excites them, but nobody signs on? A chief executive, by definition, must motivate other people to get things accomplished. A board needs a chief executive who can explain and persuade. Paid and volunteer staff need to know why they do what they do. Donors must understand the purpose and the opportunity to help financially.

Many different styles seem to work for chief executives in meeting this test. Some quietly model what they want others to see and follow. Many are particularly gifted at oral persuasion or at wielding a creative pen. A few can persuade by the sheer strength of their domineering personalities, although that is often a short-term style.

The styles that seem to last are those that put others first. They do not depend on guilt, intimidation, or obligation. They persuade by showing others that joining them is the best thing for everybody. They empower others to do their best. They are authentic in saying to others that they want to be their servant-leader. (In this compelling model, popularized by Robert K. Greenleaf in his book *Servant Leadership*, leaders lead others by serving them and helping them reach their potentials.[1])

Motivation comes after the first wave of enthusiasm. It is one thing to persuade someone to agree with you, but it requires an extra measure of skillful leadership to keep that person motivated. Being a good persuader and motivator go hand in hand.

ETHICAL

We hope ethical conduct is a universal trait of successful chief executives. The world knows the consequences of a leader with vision who persuades others to follow to society's detriment. A successful chief executive is viewed

193

What are the characteristics of the best nonprofit chief executives?

as ethical, particularly in the nonprofit world where "doing unto others" is the prime reason for existence.

Many ethical traps lurk for participants in a nonprofit organization. Sometimes a law is misunderstood; sometimes a donor tempts one to compromise in return for a gift. Friends may ask favors they shouldn't get. None of us are perfect. But people see the successful chief executive as committed to what is good and honest. When mistakes are uncovered, this type of chief executive is willing to face the music to correct what is wrong.

The best chief executives don't stop at what they perceive to be expected ethical behavior. They set the standard. They go the extra mile. They challenge board members, staff, and donors to be above reproach in all areas, and they practice what they preach. The ethical person has integrity. Once a chief executive has lost integrity in the eyes of the organization's constituents, the road back to viable leadership is a long and painful one. Thankfully, there are examples of chief executives who have traveled this road and are better people for the experience. The best ones find ways to make ethics and moral integrity their daily pursuit. One of these chief executives said, "I always act as if my 12-year-old daughter were right by my side asking me if what I'm doing is right."

FOCUSED ON STRENGTHS

Too often people feel compelled to work all the time on their weaknesses. This approach to life is promoted in some schools and many self-help books. But extensive research over many years by Donald O. Clifton, founder of Selection Research, Inc., and now chair of The Gallup Organization, Inc., shows this is a mistake. Clifton has found that the difference between just good and the best leaders is that the latter focus on their strengths and manage their weaknesses (often by delegation).[2] Our experience confirms top chief executives do not try to do all things or be all things. They focus on their strengths to achieve the productivity they enjoy.

Using this insight, these executives try to identify strengths in others and empower them to spend as much time as possible using those strengths.

The opposite approach seldom works. As Clifton's book advises, "Do not try to teach a pig to sing — it wastes your time and annoys the pig!"

DECISIVE

As the saying goes, "The buck stops here." The chief executive must be able to decide. We have seen many good leaders fail in running organizations because they simply could not make a tough call in a timely fashion.

Poor leadership sometimes results from deciding too soon. Timing is often everything. The point is that chief executives must be able to gather information, involve those who need to be involved, and then make a decision. Whether it is a quiet, personal decision following private reflection or a group decision facilitated by the chief executive, the fundamental role of good leaders is to make the call.

Management styles differ. Some visionaries reach their goals by being flexible. They keep their options open longer than others who like to come to closure much sooner. As their organizations grow, however, no decision or a late decision has a negative effect. One way to compensate for this personality type in a larger organization is to appoint a chief operating officer who makes decisions easily and put him or her in charge of daily operations. The strategic decisions are left to the chief executive, but routine decisions are someone else's responsibility.

ORGANIZED/DISCIPLINED

A chief executive who is not well organized might need to hire a good number-two person who is. Long-term success requires that programs and services be more efficient and more effective. Advancement requires a chief executive who values organization.

We are struck by the personal organization the best chief executives reflect in their personal lives. They know how to manage their schedules so that family, friends, leisure, and work are balanced. They manage their finances well enough to keep themselves and their organizations free from constant money crises. These chief executives track their work so they know when goals are reached. They delegate things others can do as well or better.

One of the most effective chief executives we have known had the uncanny ability to travel extensively and yet keep his finger on the pulse of the organization he headed. He fully understood the importance of delegating responsibility to his staff while keeping in touch with situations that needed his counsel and guiding hand. He had learned the art of being completely relaxed, as he was on the road for weeks at a time, but he had developed a system for receiving succinct reports — and information about decisions he needed to make — while he was away. This is an art more stressed-out chief executives need to develop.

Discipline in personal life carries over to discipline in organizational life. We marvel at the person who develops habits of physical fitness, spiritual growth, and intellectual stimulation, has time left for family and friends, and all the while leads a growing organization of people who are productive even when he or she is out of town. The best chief executives can do this over the long run and not burn out.

Over the years, we have found that taking time for personal and professional rejuvenation is helpful in our leadership capacities. During these productive times away from day-to-day tasks, we reflect on our responsibilities and make plans for the future. In applying this sabbatical principle to our scheduling, we take 15 to 20 minutes every day for quiet reflection, without interruption; a half day a week away from responsibilities; at least two days a month away from the desk and its duties; and, in addition to vacation or holiday time, a week or two dedicated to reflection and planning. Applying this principle keeps our spiritual and intellectual batteries charged and available for all that we face in our roles. It certainly prevents burnout.

Organization and discipline flow both from natural aptitudes and from sheer determination. This is one area where a good model — or better yet, a mentor — can help us grow.

ENERGETIC

Chief executives face unending demands in their roles: new people to meet, literature to read, travel to schedule, meetings to attend. If you are naturally endowed with high energy, you are fortunate. If not, a chief executive must learn how to generate energy through proper exercise, diet, and rest and how to conserve energy through good planning, wise decision making, and a readiness to delegate.

Our list of characteristics of effective chief executives could go on, but the ones we have described here are common to the best chief executives we know. There are always exceptions. A chief executive may get by without some of these characteristics because he or she has enough money or staff to cover mistakes. Or a chief executive is successful as a best-selling author, headline speaker, or marketing genius. Some bring such unusual assets to an organization that people willingly overlook their shortcomings. But the vast majority of those considered by their peers and constituents as being among the best will reflect the qualities we have discussed in this chapter.

SUGGESTED ACTION STEPS

1. Take inventory of your chief executive. On a scale of one to ten, what rating would you give to each of these characteristics? How can you enhance the greatest strengths?

2. When searching for a new executive, discuss whether these or other characteristics should be on your list of essentials.

3. Ask a few chief executives in the business world what characterizes success in their sector. How do those traits differ from success in the nonprofit community?

---

1. Robert K. Greenleaf, *Servant Leadership: A Journey into the Nature of Legitimate Power and Greatness* (New York: Paulist Press, 1983).

2. Donald O. Clifton and Paula Nelson, *Soar with Your Strengths* (New York: Delacorte Press, 1992).

41

Is it possible to function without naming a chief executive?

"Sometimes our chair makes the final decision, and sometimes I do."

We are intrigued by the frequency with which the question arises about running an organization without a chief executive. We believe every nonprofit organization should designate one person to function as its chief executive. That person's title does not have to include the words "chief executive" or "chief executive officer," but the bylaws and other policy documents should identify which position carries the authority and responsibility to run the organization and report to the board of directors.

Sometimes there is confusion as a result of the way terminology is applied. Many nonprofits, especially membership organizations, call their top elected volunteer "president." That role was probably filled for some time before staff was hired. The president chairs the board and carries considerable influence in these organizations. Unless the president's role is clarified and stated otherwise, the title can suggest that this person is the chief executive.

Confusion also results from the way most nonprofits are formed. Bylaws are one of the first documents written because they are requested as part of the initial application submitted to the Internal Revenue Service for exempt status. At this stage, the organization is a vision or a plan. There may be no staff. The issue of who is the chief executive is not important when there are so many other matters to address. Lacking clarification in the founding documents, the question often stays unanswered for some time.

The exception is the organization that has a definite founder who not only writes the formation documents but leaves no doubt that he or she intends to run the organization, albeit under the authority of a board (usually a group of the founder's trusted friends). The bylaws are usually clear; all other documents and activity point to this person's authority as the chief executive. Compensation is not the issue. In the early stages, this type of chief executive may function as a volunteer along with board members.

Another source of confusion over roles is the attitude that board members and staff work as a team and don't want to put one person on a pedestal. This value system, in our opinion, is misguided but nevertheless present in some organizations. More often than not, a subtle competition for authority takes place among several people on the board and staff, and organizational matters suffer.

WHY HAVE A DESIGNATED CHIEF EXECUTIVE?

From one perspective, the job of a chief executive is impossible. But from another, it is impossible to have a well-functioning organization without one person functioning as the chief executive. As we urge throughout this book, servant-leadership reflects the best model of chief executive behavior. It is not a power game or a question of who can boss whom. It is not even necessarily a question of who gets the highest salary. Naming someone to function as the chief executive has everything to do with effectiveness, efficiency, productivity, high morale, and order. A good chief executive must

199

Is it possible to function without naming a chief executive?

delegate. But nearly every nonprofit organization needs one chief executive. There are a number of good reasons why.

- *A board needs one agent.* In earlier chapters we laid out key responsibilities of a nonprofit board. Recall that policy is always set by group action. No board member has more authority than other board members when it comes to establishing organizational policy. When policy is set, it is important that everyone knows who is responsible for implementing it. You can imagine the confusion that would result if a board tried to parcel out assignments among many board members, paid staff, or volunteers.

  The chief executive also serves as the bridge between board and staff, whether paid or volunteer. He or she works closely with the board chair in setting board agendas and coordinating the staff work the board requires to do its job.

- *The staff needs to know where the buck stops.* Competition among staff to determine who is in charge is distracting, if not destructive. Even when the chief paid staff person is known, some think the chief executive is really the chair of the board. They are tempted to make end runs on the chief executive if they believe someone else could make or change an executive decision.

- *Donors need to identify the leader.* Donors enjoy giving to successful organizations. Many like to interact personally with the chief executive. People who give need confidence that the organization is in good hands—usually, one set of hands.

- *Other external constituencies need to know who's in charge.* In organizational life, some things simply need the attention of the one person responsible for the whole. Banks, insurance companies, vendors, and others need the signature of the chief executive. Amazingly, we often see different people — usually the chair and the chief staff executive — pass the ball back and forth when it comes to representing the administration of a nonprofit corporation. Such an organization may be functioning legally, but it is always better to sort out roles in advance rather than force people to deal with shifting authority.

- *Planning needs a facilitator.* The chief executive is the natural person to coordinate an organization's planning process. Even when the board takes an active role and there are senior staff to do much of the work, planning breaks down without a chief executive to lead and to provide the continuity from planning to action.

- *The organization needs one spokesperson.* Public relations is important to most nonprofits. Although larger organizations may have a staff member with daily responsibility for this area, the policy and the tone of what is distributed to the media and the public need clarity and continuity. If your organization has ever had a well-publicized change or crisis, you know how important it is not to have several people trying to explain to the world what is happening. Although we earlier described when the board chair serves as a public spokesperson, the chief executive normally fills that role.

EXCEPTIONS TO THE RULE

The nature or complexity of some nonprofit organizations may call for designating two chief executives. Generally, these twin responsibilities make sense when the organization is keyed to an area of service that requires a highly skilled and visible professional person — a symphony orchestra conductor, a senior pastor, an educational leader—and a highly skilled executive administrator.

Personalities are key to making this cooperative model work. We know of an organization in which the board gave authority for content leadership to one gifted person (who dislikes administration) and authority for budget, personnel, and related matters to another gifted person with a business background (who loves administration). We think local churches of more than 25 staff should consider this model. It is difficult in the long run for a pastor to function as the senior executive.

The usual answer to the need for content and administrative skills is that one is named chief executive and the other fills a number-two position. This model — not dual leadership — is probably the best one for most organizations. Whatever model you choose, don't lose sight of the key principle: Everyone must be clear on who has executive authority for what.

Figure 9

Differentiating between the Chief Executive and Chief Operating Officers

CEO	COO
The leader	The manager
Doing the right things	Doing things right
Focuses on long view	Focuses on short view
Focuses on what and why	Focuses on how
Has/inspires others with vision	Has hands-on control
Thinks future	Thinks present
Innovation, development	Administration
Sets tone, direction	Sets the pace
Relates to COO and outside	Relates to CEO and inside
Accountable to a board	Accountable to the CEO

SUGGESTED ACTION STEPS

1. Check the organization's bylaws to see whether the designation of a chief executive is explicit.

2. If you have always considered the volunteer board chair, not the senior staff officer, to be the chief executive, consider whether time and circumstances might require changing that system in the future.

3. If you are one of the few organizations in which a dual executive model should be considered, ask the board to discuss the pros and cons.

4. Use Figure 9 to evaluate how your chief executive could or should complement a chief operating officer.

42

How should a board evaluate its chief executive?

"I was fired by my board out of the blue. No one on the board even hinted that I wasn't doing a good job. I'm frustrated and angry."

As we wrote this chapter, our schedules for the week included appointments with two chief executives who had just been fired and another who knew it was coming in a week or two. One went to the final board meeting thinking he was going to get a good raise. Another had been evaluated by a small committee of the board and was told orally that he was doing a good job and would likely receive a raise. The third had not received a formal evaluation in several years.

Why is it that boards are so poor at evaluating their chief executives? Why don't chief executives have a better read on how their boards really perceive them? Why do so few boards have procedures in place to build a better relationship with the person who should be their greatest asset?

For one thing, many boards have never spelled out the goals for their organization against which the chief executive's leadership could be evaluated. Some chief executives resist setting specific performance objectives and then seeking board approval. Most volunteer board members feel uncomfortable discussing their differences with the chief executive, particularly if he or she recruited them to the board.

All staff (and board members) should be able to answer five basic questions about their individual jobs:

1. What am I expected to do?
2. Why is it important?
3. Do I have authority to do it?
4. When I need help, where can I go?
5. How am I doing so far?

Organizational effectiveness and individual well-being suffer when these questions are not clearly answered.

WHY EVALUATE THE CHIEF EXECUTIVE?

A staff member's answer to "How am I doing so far?" can often be inferred from day-to-day interaction, even in the absence of a formal evaluation program. This is not true for the chief executive, who has many "bosses" and frequently gets inadequate and even conflicting signals by trying to read board members' minds. Why should a board conduct a planned, thoughtful evaluation of its chief executive? Here are three good reasons:

- *For the board:* Determining evaluation criteria makes everyone focus on the same assumptions about the organization's direction and priorities.

- *For the chief executive:* A good evaluation process offers protection from being judged (or even fired) based on personality differences rather than on accomplishments.

- *For other staff:* When the board and chief executive agree on their priorities, staff members usually receive clearer directions for their work and their own performance evaluations.

In the final analysis, the chief executive should be held accountable for everything accomplished by staff and volunteers. When he or she is fuzzy about what the board expects, the whole organization may lack focus, suffer low morale, and consequently be less effective. A good performance evaluation process for the chief executive focuses the board's expectations. Indeed, it may even serve as (but not substitute for) a useful strategic planning or evaluation process.

Of course, every chief executive is evaluated constantly in the minds of board members, staff, volunteers, donors, and beneficiaries of the organization's services. But when there are no common assumptions about the evaluation criteria and no process for articulating the unspoken, a chief executive risks a lot by not insisting upon a periodic evaluation. Our advice to prospective chief executives is this: Do not accept a position until you are sure of the criteria on which you will be evaluated and have a board commitment to complete an annual evaluation with you. Otherwise, you may face the unhappy experience many chief executives have suffered — a surprise termination based on a difference of style with a few board members.

HOW TO EVALUATE

There are many kinds of evaluations, ranging from a short conversation with board officers to a full-blown assessment that uses an outside consultant to interview board members, staff, donors, and others.[1] What is right for your organization is usually evident once the board chair and the chief executive agree on a general approach. Here are some tips:

- The board and the chief executive should develop the process and timing together.
- Separate the evaluation process from salary negotiations, which should come later.
- The board should not evaluate any staff other than the chief executive.
- Use a two- to three-member ad hoc committee of skilled board members to conduct the evaluation.

- As the situation requires it, decide whether to interview staff. Note: This should rarely be necessary and happen only with the chief executive's knowledge.

- Give the entire board an oral report after debriefing the chief executive.

- Write an "evaluation of the evaluation" for the files so the process can be even more effective the next time.

WHAT TO EVALUATE

The board should evaluate all aspects of the chief executive's performance in helping the organization accomplish the expectations the board has established. (This is difficult to do if the board has not been clear in setting the organization's mission.) Board evaluation committees commonly ask whether the chief executive's leadership has accomplished these goals:

- Created positive relationships with board members and helped strengthen the board;

- Built a strong internal organization in which systems, staff productivity and morale, and teamwork have improved;

- Advanced the quality and increased the quantity of the services provided;

- Increased the public's trust in the organization's integrity; and

- Improved financial resources and accountability.

A good evaluation process should also:

- Allow the entire board to help create a customized evaluation form with both quantifiable and open-ended questions;

- Allow the chief executive to write a self-evaluation as part of the process;

- Give the chief executive an opportunity to discuss items to be sure of accurate interpretation of the board's conclusions, both positive and negative; and

- Provide time at the end to write mutually agreed-upon performance criteria for the next year's evaluation.

Everyone benefits from an evaluation process that is sensitively conducted. While boards that are not accustomed to evaluation may feel uncomfortable at first, the positive results of honesty and sincerity inevitably lead to a better organization and a more productive relationship with the chief executive. As in any relationship, open communication improves the level of trust and the ability to work in harmony.

SUGGESTED ACTION STEPS

1. Read the resources listed in the notes for this chapter.

2. If the board doesn't know about the facts of evaluation, the chief executive or the board chair should inform them — for example, about what the bylaws or board policies say, what the chief executive was told when hired, and when the last formal evaluation was completed.

3. Ask the board to brainstorm for 15 minutes about why an evaluation is good and how it could be done best. Ask the chair to appoint three interested, knowledgeable board members to use that information and draft a procedure and timetable for evaluation.

---

1. Jane Pierson and Joshua Mintz, *Assessment of the Chief Executive: A Tool for Boards and Chief Executives of Nonprofit Organizations* (Washington, DC: National Center for Nonprofit Boards [now BoardSource], 1995); Brian O'Connell, "Recruiting, Encouraging, and Evaluating the Chief Staff Officer," chap. 8 in *The Board Member's Book*, 2nd ed. (New York: Foundation Center, 1993).

43

How do we set fair compensation for our chief executive and staff?

"People shouldn't expect to make much money working for a nonprofit."

Compensation in the nonprofit arena was a fairly quiet, noncontroversial topic until February 16, 1992. On that day the *Washington Post* ran a front-page story about the $463,000 salary of William Aramony, then president of United Way of America. That story brought the compensation issue into the limelight.

The many news stories that ensued about salaries and benefits in the nonprofit sector paralleled similar stories in 1992 and 1993 about corporate executives. In both sectors, the need for boards to take more seriously the issue of reasonable salaries has been heightened. One series in the *Philadelphia Inquirer* reported that at least 1,000 nonprofit chief executives had salaries exceeding that of the president of the United States, and some made more than $1 million a year.

But let's get back to reality. Extremely high salaries are rare. They apply to huge tax-exempt nonprofit organizations with billion-dollar budgets. They are not generally found in the 500,000 or so "average" nonprofits whose budgets seldom exceed a few million dollars. Our focus here is on these organizations, which form the vast majority of the nonprofit sector. They may have one or two paid staff or several hundred. Usually their boards want to be competitive but not exceed the salary guidelines of other similar organizations. Few nonprofit professionals get paid as much as those doing similar work in the business community.

How should compensation decisions be made? Here are some practical questions to ask when setting guidelines:

- *What is our financial strength?* You can't pay more than you have. Payroll and program costs must be in a reasonable balance to fulfill your charitable purpose. You should have a reserve account of at least 10 to 12 percent of your operating budget so you can pay salaries when cash flow is down. If you are struggling financially, you may not be able to pay what the salary surveys say is average.

- *What is our philosophy about compensation?* It is wise for the board to reflect on what kind of nonprofit entity it governs and how donors and moral owners feel about compensation in your sector. Staff in social services organizations, for example, seldom make what their counterparts do in health organizations. Donors to religious organizations do not expect employees to earn what business trade associations might pay. Once the board realizes what is publicly acceptable, however, it still needs to determine philosophically whether it would like its employees to be near the mean, the median, or in the upper quarter of similar organizations.

- *What can we learn from salary surveys?* Your chief executive is probably aware of a few national and regional surveys conducted by nonprofit associations or private firms.[1] They are useful, but the sample size and type influence the results. Usually, salaries are reported according to budget and staff size. The "average" chief executive salary reported in one may be almost twice the average reported in another. Naturally, salaries in major metropolitan areas are higher than salaries in less urban regions. People reporting to chief executives make anywhere from 50 to 85 percent of what the chief executives make. In 1999, using rough averages, nearly half of all nonprofit chief executives made less than $55,000 in salary, and over 80 percent of them earned less than $80,000.

• *What is our goal?* Some boards decide salaries are less than what they would like them to be. They set a goal — say, to have salaries reflect approximately 80 percent of salaries in similar jobs in the local business market. It may take three years or more to reach this goal, but board members and staff could be motivated to find the financial means to meet it. In addition, a board should have this kind of framework within which to plan.

• *Does the board determine specific salaries other than for the chief executive?* There are exceptions, but we generally feel comfortable in saying the board should set the chief executive's compensation and let him or her, within board guidelines, determine the rest of the payroll. The chief executive is in the best position to know what it takes to recruit and keep good people. Staff should feel that someone who knows their work is setting their compensation.

• *What about performance-based compensation?* We like the trend of tying salaries and/or bonuses to performance. While there are no solid figures available, more and more nonprofits are adopting this practice. So-called merit pay is more complicated than salaries adjusted periodically as the need requires. Some feel it creates too much competition and not enough teamwork. The board should set some guidelines. Should you consider bonuses for work groups in addition to, or instead of, individual performance ratings? Should cost-of-living adjustments be dropped entirely? Should performance pay increase the base salary or be paid in one-time, lump-sum bonuses? Approximately what percentage of staff, roughly, should get performance raises? By how much should the highest merit increase exceed the smallest merit increase? These are all value judgments a good chief executive will explore, with some broad policies from the board.

Merit-based compensation can work well under the following conditions:

1. The staff has a role in deciding the pros and cons.

2. The board supports the efforts and monitors the results.

3. The criteria for awarding bonuses are generally understood.

4. Merit pay is a small part of the total compensation program.

5. The board uses the same approach with the chief executive.

If staff are involved in creating a system of rewarding performance, they may be more open to the idea that those who go the extra mile should be rewarded, or that measuring performance is a good strategy for accomplishing the organization's mission. They may agree that people should be allowed to compete for something extra in a nonprofit organization that pays modest salaries. It takes a skilled chief executive to process this staff discussion. Facilitation by an outside consultant may be worth the expense.

- *What besides cash should be explored in compensation?* From the board's perspective, the total outlay for employees should be more important than how benefits are distributed. For the chief executive in particular, it may be more important to keep salary lower in order to meet individual needs more creatively through additional health and life insurance, deferred compensation, coverage of educational expenses, an annual executive physical exam, a study leave, or use of a vehicle.

211

How do we set fair compensation for our chief executive and staff?

Compensation is a difficult area for some boards, but it is a major responsibility. Too many organizations have out-of-date, perhaps unfair, compensation systems. At the minimum, it is important for the chief executive and board to work together on general policies and on annual reviews of the chief executive (see Chapter 42). Remember the organization's mission demands effective leadership, not just average management — and that requires a financial investment.

On the other hand, the board needs to pay attention to over compensation. The 1996 Intermediate Sanctions allow the IRS to set heavy penalties on board members and managers who approve or receive unreasonable compensation for their work or service.

SUGGESTED ACTION STEPS

1. Ask the chief executive to gather and summarize for the board facts and trends about staff compensation in your field. (Most chief executives will welcome that kind of request.)

2. Identify the five nonprofit organizations most comparable to your own. Then request copies (from them or the IRS) of their most recent Form 990s so you can compare compensation levels.

3. Research and purchase for board education one of the national compensation surveys.

4. Invite two or three outside experts to review your current policies and practices and make recommendations to the board.

---

1. Nonprofits often use two annual national surveys: *Compensation in Nonprofit Organizations,* conducted by Abbott, Langer & Associates, Crete, IL (708-672-4200), and *Association Executives Compensation Study,* conducted by the American Society of Association Executives, Washington, DC (202-626-2742).

How do we find a new chief executive?

*"I think choosing a good chief executive
is the board's primary function."*

Appointing a good chief executive is truly a key task for any board. We are surprised at how casual some boards are in their search for a chief executive officer. There are entire books written on the search process, but we offer some of the basics here.[1]

When the previous chief executive departs with little advance notice, some organizations move too quickly, believing they must fill the slot as soon as possible. We have seen many mistakes in this approach. It is extremely important to step back, assess the state of the organization, plan the search, and then conduct it well. This chapter describes the key steps.

1. Conduct a presearch assessment.

The full board or executive committee should review at least the following:

- mission and goals;

- staff morale and needs;
- current programmatic needs of the organization;
- constituency support;
- financial condition; and
- previous chief executive's experience.

2. Prepare a profile of desired characteristics.

It is prudent to ask a number of people (staff, board members, major donors, and leaders in your sector) what characteristics a new chief executive should have for the current stage in the organization's life cycle. Once you focus on particular candidates, it is difficult to be objective. But it is extremely important to define what you need before getting into personalities. At a minimum, the board should sign off on a description of the desired competencies, character, personality, and experience a new chief executive should have.

3. Write a position description.

The chief executive of any organization is asked to achieve the intended results within the policy parameters set by the board. But candidates will want to see what the board expects the chief executive to accomplish, how the position relates to the board, and what the specific duties are. We can think of several key appointments where no discussion took place about the board's style in governing the organization. The result was a short tenure. It is imperative that a prospective chief executive understand and agree with the board's expectations for how their roles work together to accomplish the organization's mission.

4. Manage the search.

A good method is to form a committee that manages the executive search and makes recommendations to the board. Using a search committee invites wide participation, builds ownership in the decision, and allows board and staff to collaborate on a decision critical to both groups. The board must be clear in its mandate to the committee, giving it a timetable, a budget, an explanation of its authority, and an idea of how many candidates to present to the board. Committee members may come only from the board, but they can also represent the organization's constituency and staff. A good chair ensures that the process is fair and well organized and stays on track.

A staff coordinator is essential to the work of the search committee. The coordinator manages the logistics of the search, creates candidate files, and organizes committee meetings. This person must be able to maintain the strict confidentiality required during the search.

Depending on the organization's size, complexity, and resources, some boards use an executive search firm. These firms generally charge a fee ranging from 30 to 35 percent of the chief executive's compensation, plus expenses. Several good search firms specialize in sectors of the nonprofit community. It is helpful when board members have experience in selecting and working with a search firm. Once a firm is chosen, an account executive will lead the process we describe here. We believe a good search firm is worth the extra cost if there are no obvious candidates known, the search is national or international, and time is of the essence.

An external search for a chief executive can easily take from four to five months, even longer in colleges or universities and other complex organizations where several constituencies must be involved and the search is national or international.

5. Identify candidates.

Our experience is that most chief executives did not apply directly for the job (although sometimes they heard about the job and asked to be nominated). Top people are often satisfied with their current jobs and are contacted because someone nominated them without their knowledge. Contacting a broad group of people who know good prospects is the primary way to build a list of candidates. A letter inviting nominations, sent to several hundred key constituents and leaders in the field by the board chair or the search committee chair, is well worth the effort. Well-placed ads can also help get the word out. As applicants and nominees become known, they should be sent an attractive information package with documents on the organization's mission and goals and the desired qualifications of a new chief executive. Included in that package is a request for a letter of interest, a resume, and the names of references. As these materials come in, the search committee can begin reviewing them.

6. Narrow the field.

Developing clear criteria before the search will prepare the way for evaluating candidate files. When the announced deadline is past, you will begin to narrow the field to a short list of three to seven candidates. (Never set an absolute deadline because you do not want to close out a good possibility.) Then call these individuals to ask whether they wish to be considered active candidates. Some of them may be happily situated in their current positions and need more information about what your organization has to offer. You want candidates who are drawn to your mission after studying your materials. And you should expect a challenge in winning the interest of some good nominees.

7. Conduct reference checks and interviews.

Depending on time, distance, and funding, candidates on the short list are typically screened at length by phone after a few reference checks confirm their attractiveness. Good questions should be thoughtfully selected in advance and given to the search committee members who make the phone calls. We don't think any candidate should make it to the final two before thorough phone conversations with more than one search committee member, six to eight reference checks, perhaps a credit check, and a personal interview. There are many different ways of working during these final stages of a search. The key is to keep the process moving and to be thorough. Remember: The best time to fire a chief executive is before you hire one.

8. Negotiate with the selected candidate.

Care in presenting a written offer is a wise and necessary procedure. When the board and the new chief executive make oral agreements, too many assumptions result, and uncomfortable situations can arise later. We counsel boards to let the chief executive-designate have a few days to review the draft appointment document, which will be signed by both parties, and suggest changes. It is too easy to get caught up in the emotions of an imminent appointment and overlook important issues that are easier to deal with now than six months into the job.

9. Announce the appointment and begin the transition.

Once a decision has been made, it is important to contact those close to the organization, including key moral owners and participants in the search process. A special introduction to the staff and a media release are appropriate. Once the decision is announced, the search coordinator can send letters to the other candidates, clean out and secure the files, pay outstanding bills, and write thank-you notes to all those who helped.

The board chair and a senior staff member should help ease the outgoing and new chief executive through the transition period. If the new leader is moving from another city, the list of things to do is long indeed. Sometimes the appointment does not take effect for several months. Most new chief executives want to be informed and consulted on key issues even before they arrive for the first day of work. How the board and staff begin building their professional relationship with the new chief executive during this stage has a lot to do with his or her long-term success.

We have only scratched the surface in dealing with the search for a new chief executive. Thankfully, there is good reference material about this process. Board members in other similar organizations are another valuable resource. Even if you are not involved in a search today, we encourage you to consider the action steps that follow.

SUGGESTED ACTION STEPS

1. Develop a policy on selecting a new chief executive now, before the need arises and as part of overall policymaking. It can be better thought out in calm than in crisis.

2. Ask the chair to have a conversation with your current chief executive about his or her plans for the future. This could be a routine question in the annual evaluation. Try to anticipate the timing and circumstances of a needed search.

3. Assign the board development committee or an ad hoc task force to research the topic of executive searches so that a good file is available when needed.

---

1. Two excellent sources of information are the National Center for Nonprofit Boards [now BoardSource] (*Hiring the Chief Executive* by Sheila Albert) and the Association of Governing Boards of Universities and Colleges (One Dupont Circle, NW, Suite 400, Washington, DC 20036; 800-356-6317).

45

What is the chief executive's role in improving the board?

*"Some days I don't know whether the board
leads me or I lead the board!"*

Clear and open communication between the board and chief executive is critical. In the traditional hierarchical model for the board-executive relationship, the board runs the organization and the chief executive serves the board. Certainly, the board holds both legal and moral responsibility for the ultimate state of affairs in a nonprofit organization, but this model never fully works in practice. Then there is the too-familiar situation of the chief executive running everything, using the board as a friendly advisory group or just a rubber stamp. This model is dangerous; recall the Foundation for New Era Philanthropy, in which some board members named by the chief executive didn't even remember they were on the board. No chief executive should aspire to have all the authority with only a token board.

If neither of these models works, what is the answer? In their interesting analysis of effective nonprofits, Robert D. Herman and Richard D. Heimovics found an alternative model.[1] This model says (our paraphrase) good nonprofits have good boards, and boards are good when they have a chief executive who helps them be good.

Except on rare occasions, this model works best. The chief executive needs to have a board-centered leadership style. There should be no competition between board and staff. The chief executive must help the board be strong without worrying that he or she is giving up authority. Herman and Heimovics list six skills of the board-centered executive:

1. Facilitating interaction in board relationships;
2. Showing consideration and respect toward board members;
3. Envisioning change and innovation with the board;
4. Promoting board accomplishments and productivity;
5. Initiating and maintaining a structure for board work;
6. Providing helpful information to the board.[2]

We agree with board-centered leadership for the chief executive. A proper balance must be struck between the board doing its work independently and the other extreme, in which the chief executive forges ahead, almost neglecting the board. As in all human interaction, trust is key. The board needs to perceive that the chief executive is sincerely helping them to be all that a good board should be.

For certain, no board can be effective when it feels it is competing with the chief executive and not getting the support it needs. So the chief executive needs to make developing the board a priority. This takes time. Some successful chief executives say as much as 20 percent of their time is devoted to board relations. Does this sound like a lot? Count the hours spent nurturing prospective board members, orienting new members, meeting individually with the chair and other board members, preparing for meetings, and doing the follow-up every board meeting requires. We encourage chief executives to view these hours as some of the most important they give to the organization.

We urge chief executives who are not now board-centered to move quickly in that direction. By helping empower the board in its legitimate functions, they will strengthen themselves as chief executives. Trust will develop, and the board will move away from its tendencies to micromanage or function mostly as a watchdog. The chief executive will help them focus on mission, goals, and standing policies that give direction, but not on unjustified control.

One question chief executives always ask is whether they should be members of the board. We addressed this question in Chapter 38. We repeat here that regardless of whether they are board members, chief executives will likely have more influence on board decisions than any single member because of their knowledge and experience. But we do feel it is appropriate for most chief executives (and no other staff) to be on the board ex officio (by virtue of position) without vote. The chief executive's task is to be a faithful implementer of the board's policy, regardless of personal feelings (which should have been freely shared in the discussion leading to the vote).

Trying to lead a board and still be its primary employee can be tricky. One's attitude must always be that of a servant-leader, whether working with the board or with the staff. From our experience, these are the best ways for a chief executive to give leadership:

- *Be a student of nonprofit governance.* No other staff or board member is likely to be as motivated to learn common principles and emerging trends related to boards. Many good, recent resources on board issues are available. For general purposes, the best come from BoardSource (formerly the National Center for Nonprofit Boards). Nearly every major association offers workshops for chief executives and board members. We hope this book is only one of several that chief executives will use in providing board leadership.

- *Train the board*. No one should take for granted that board members, even experienced ones, are working under the same assumptions about the board's role. Most members have been on several nonprofit boards. They bring differing opinions about what the board should or should not do. Each organization must develop written policies regarding how it does its governing tasks. The chief executive should be instrumental in helping the board reach consensus positions on a range of structural and role issues. Orientation for new board members is only the first opportunity in a broader training program.

- *Help shape standing policies*. We've all sat in meetings where one board member throws out a 100-word motion that is discussed and passed, only to discover later that (a) no one put the actual motion into writing or (b) when the minutes are read at the next meeting, there are three different views of what really happened. The chief executive should anticipate from the agenda prepared with the board chair what critical issues will require board action. When a draft motion is carefully articulated and distributed in writing, the board can deal with it much more thoughtfully. Even with a few amendments, it will become part of the policy manual and stand the test of time.

- *Help recruit new board members*. It takes more than brainstorming for an hour every year to come up with the right people for the board. The chief executive has the most at stake in finding qualified people who know enough about the organization to make a wise decision about serving as a board member. Good chief executives keep a list in the side drawer and pull people into the organization's volunteer activities who might later be considered for board service.

- *Insist on board-friendly staff reports*. What works best for staff often does not work best for boards. Chief executives can facilitate the governance process by helping staff develop reports and issue papers that suit the needs of volunteer board members. Materials should be in context and as brief as possible. They should explain pros and cons, present a clear recommendation if called for, and respond to board concerns expressed in the past. Little things make a difference.

There are other ways board-centered chief executives help lead their boards. Many are covered in other chapters. But don't get lost in the details. The key point is all boards require leadership from their chief executive to do their work well. As we often say to chief executives, "A strong board can become your greatest legacy."

SUGGESTED ACTION STEPS

1. Commit to reading new governance resource materials for five hours next month.

2. Have lunch with your chair to discuss how you, the chief executive, can help the board become better.

3. Host a staff brainstorming session on how you could help improve the board.

---

1. Robert D. Herman and Richard D. Heimovics, *Executive Leadership in Nonprofit Organizations: New Strategies for Shaping Executive-Board Dynamics* (San Francisco: Jossey-Bass, 1991).

2. Ibid., p. 117.

46

How can all senior staff contribute to board effectiveness?

"The chief executive seems to exclude senior staff too much."

Senior staff have a critical role in helping the board do its work well. We believe the chief executive is the sole agent of the board to implement its policies. But all professional staff play key roles in helping both the chief executive and the board.

Should staff other than the chief executive attend board meetings? We believe they should. They hear firsthand the concerns of the board. They see how their boss explains the issues. They are available to answer questions from board members when asked by the chief executive. They can often be of personal assistance to board members during breaks. And being in the boardroom reduces some of the mystery and anxiety about the governance process. Staff see that board members are quite ordinary people doing their best to help fulfill the mission.

After the board meeting, the chief executive benefits from hearing the perspectives of each staff member. When the board has made significant policy changes, the key people know the importance of adjusting to the new direction because they were present for the board discussion. They are better able to explain board actions to their own staffs.

So what are the negative aspects of staff attending board meetings? Frankly, there are none — if the staff realize they are not board members and do not try to enter into board discussions. We suggest that staff, other than the chief executive, not sit at the board table during business sessions. This physical separation helps reinforce the distinction between roles.

The role of staff in governance-related work goes well beyond board meetings. Here are the primary ways staff make a difference:

- *Good reports.* We all know the hard work that goes into preparing for board meetings. Good written reports from senior staff, sent to the full board a couple of weeks in advance of their meetings, educate board members and prepare them for dialogue. Reports should be clear, put issues in context, and indicate how board policies are working.

- *Tracking systems.* The board should identify how it will determine whether staff are reaching key goals. Usually, staff are asked to help create tracking measures. Good data are essential to good governance. Staff can either hide useful information by submerging it in lengthy reports, or they can display it in a timely and understandable manner to enhance board decisions.

- *Committee staff work.* Many boards have committees that relate closely to one or more senior staff assignments. Staff naturally become the primary resource for committee chairs as they plan agendas or prepare special reports. In this way, staff can help committees focus on board issues, not staff responsibilities.

- *Response to inquiries.* Board officers and committee chairs often need information between meetings. While board members should not ask staff to produce information that is primarily of personal interest, responding to board inquiries is part of the job. We believe all requests for staff help should come through the chief executive. However, senior staff often have the task of pulling together information that fulfills the request. This is yet another way to be clear, timely, and helpful to board work.

- *Staff teamwork.* Board members observe how well their staff get along, work together, and are loyal to the mission and one another. Staff who "end run" their chief executives, betray confidences to board members during informal conversations, or talk negatively about their colleagues do not help the cause. Staff need to earn the board's trust through consistent professional behavior that reflects a quality staff team.

- *Relationship building.* Social exchanges between individual senior staff and board members can be another healthy way to build board effectiveness. Showing interest in a board member's personal or professional life is one simple way to honor that person. Being willing to go the extra mile to help out on a personal need is another. Senior staff and board members can have meaningful friendships as long as they are not used inappropriately when it comes to the work of the organization.

- *Lead by modeling.* Everyone knows committees are meant to help the board — not the staff — do its work, but old habits can be hard to break. Committees, especially, can fall into the trap of advising a staff member while neglecting to formulate policy recommendations for board action. Staff need to model the policy governance process by not encouraging board members or committees to compromise their job descriptions. Staff can get advice from anywhere, including some board members, but that activity needs to fall outside of governance work.

- *Board member nominations.* While the board itself is responsible for defining and identifying good board prospects, senior staff often know volunteers and donors who could be considered. The board should encourage this advice from its staff.

You can think of other ways staff are critical to good governance. The main point to remember is that these capable, dedicated people can and should contribute to the board's work. Staff and board are not in competition. When each group understands the potential for positive interaction and works to make the other stronger and more effective, they advance the organization's mission.

SUGGESTED ACTION STEPS

1. Ask the board or executive committee to give the chief executive their thoughts on how the senior staff is, or is not, being used to advance the work of the board.

2. The chief executive could ask senior staff to evaluate their own attitudes about and experience with board relations, coming to consensus on how to improve.

47

How does a chief executive know when it's time to step down?

"I want to be one of the first to know when I've outlived my effectiveness in this organization."

Lowell had been chief executive of a health services clinic for nine years. He was not the founder, but he had brought the organization through its greatest growth period. With a few exceptions, his board had always backed him. Staff were generally supportive. The budget was in good shape. But for several months he has had a nagging question: "Have I been here long enough?"

Lowell's question can't be answered by anyone but Lowell, given his fairly positive situation. But the general question is one chief executives discuss among themselves. They want to know how to recognize the signals that it might be time to move on. We offer the common responses for your consideration here.

What is the average tenure of a chief executive in the nonprofit sector? We have not seen reliable data on the sector at large, but five to 10 years

228
NONPROFIT BOARD ANSWER BOOK

seems to be a reasonable estimate. There are well over one million nonprofit chief executives out there. That means perhaps more than 150,000 left their chief executive roles in the last year. How did they reach this decision?

Most chief executives prefer to decide to leave before their boards ask them to leave. In our experience, some turnover is due to board firings or requests for resignation. Unfortunately, these occasions are often painful for everyone. The staff, the board, and the departing chief executive need time to overcome the emotions of anger, frustration, doubt, guilt, and anxiety. We hope that some of the chapters in Part III will help boards improve the way they deal with their chief executives.

If you have been a chief executive for a while, you are the rare leader who, even if only on those few bad days, does not think privately that it may be time to leave. Our advice is: Don't dwell on it. Be honest with yourself when the thoughts recur. Acknowledge the normal cycle of birth and death, creating and ending, starting and finishing. In these times, a chief executive staying in one place for 20 years or more is a rarity.

We suggest you ask yourself some of these questions when you feel in the mood to assess where you are in your career:

- *Have you fulfilled all the major goals you were hired to accomplish?* Sometimes a chief executive is hired for particular skills that fit particular needs of an organization at a point in time. When those needs or projects are past, perhaps the organization needs a different type of leadership for its next phase. The question is worth asking, even though we believe most chief executives are challenged by regularly creating new goals and helping the organization achieve them.

- *Have you lost your earlier passion for your work?* A chief executive needs a certain amount of passion to stay in the top leadership post. He or she is the keeper of the vision. Others, particularly volunteers, look to the chief executive for their own continuing motivation to serve the organization. There are many reasons one might lose passion. There are short periods when the intensity of passion is lost but then returns.

Renewal is always possible. Only honest introspection will bring the question to the surface, although the process may be triggered by the observations of close friends.

- *Are you bored most of the time?* Some chief executives have simply mastered the job of an organization whose board wants a maintenance-type operation. Because we believe a chief executive must constantly be learning and growing, both personally and professionally, boredom is a warning sign. Look first at changing the situation to allow growth. But boredom may be a signal to look elsewhere.

- *Are your ideas resisted more than welcomed?* To lead, you need people who generally welcome your ideas. We know chief executives whose ideas no longer elicit the excitement they once did. Sometimes the chief executive's leanings move him or her beyond the boundaries of acceptable practice with the board. Or staff can challenge the direction a chief executive wants to go. Whatever the reasons, increasing resistance to your ideas is another signal that your contribution is nearing an end.

- *Has your key constituency moved away from the organization?* Sometimes a chief executive is recruited and supported heavily by a group of people who make the job exciting — board members, staff, major donors, alumni leaders, or others. When these people change their focus to other areas or leave your team, it may be time to reassess. You may have others who support you, but changing the dynamic of your front line alters the formula for bold leadership.

- *Have the politics of your environment left you wounded?* Even when chief executives do not contribute to political battles, many are caught up in them. Sometimes peace can result only through a change in leadership. Some chief executives feel forced to choose sides in a divisive struggle within the board or among key donors or partner organizations. Whatever the history of these stressful times, the chief executive may need to move on so scars can heal. First consider whether staying is even more important, a decision that should be confirmed by board members, staff, and others who continue as strong players.

- *Have you mentored younger leaders who are ready to succeed you?* We have older chief executive friends who prepared one or more colleagues to take over some day, subject to the board's wishes. In most situations, this is an admirable trait of a good leader. Does the leader recognize that moment when the junior colleague is ready and may move on if impatient with the wait? Clear understanding between the board and the chief executive about succession planning is critical.

- *Is your annual board evaluation giving mixed messages?* Boards have a hard time being honest with their chief executives when a number of board members think it is time for a change. It is common to gloss over these doubts when giving feedback after an evaluation. Often this situation can continue for a few years before the board confronts the chief executive with the question of resignation. A chief executive must encourage honest feedback and be careful to read between the lines of any evaluation that sends mixed messages.

- *Are family members or close friends giving clear signals to leave?* Much of our identity is bound up in our work. It is not easy to give up the title "chief executive" when everything seems to be going well. But a balanced life outside of work is important, too. We encourage chief executives to be open and honest with family, particularly spouses, and friends so they can give helpful counsel. If that counsel is, "It's time to move on," you should take it seriously.

- *Have you lost your credibility to lead?* Once you have lost your credibility — most often tied to your integrity — it is time to leave for the good of the organization. Almost always, someone who has lost the integrity battle is unable to continue in the same job successfully. It takes a change of environment for the process of restoration and renewal to work.

- *Were serious misrepresentations made during the hiring process?* Although this question is not the most important one, you should ask it if you feel defeated, overwhelmed, or bitter because the board did not level with you. Once on the job, you discovered that the leadership task was quite different from what had been portrayed. If this unfortunate scenario fits, even though you may have completed only a few months, it may be wise to leave if you cannot adjust to the new understanding of the job.

- *Do you have a legitimate "call" to another role?* It is common for chief executives to feel a special calling to their roles. A feeling of inner peace usually accompanies such a decision, which can even happen when a chief executive is quite happy in his or her current position. More often, however, the moment arrives after answering the questions we have outlined here in the affirmative. We believe many of our chief executive friends were legitimately called to their leadership roles. This is most often a key factor in religious organizations. We also hope they are open to knowing when the release from the call occurs. It may or may not be when another call comes along.

A word of caution: On down days, you might feel like answering "yes" to several of the above questions. We urge you to resist quick conclusions. We hope most chief executives are affirmed by this chapter in continuing to provide strong leadership in the job they are in. But it is a useful exercise to sort through difficult questions that may tell you when to go.

SUGGESTED ACTION STEPS

1. In two or three pages, assess your feelings and make an objective analysis of your contributions to the organization. Put the document away for 30 days. Then get away from the office for a few hours to review and revise it. Did your first analysis hold up, or did it reflect only one point in time?

2. If you sincerely feel the urge to move on, test it out first with family, then close friends outside the organization, and then with your board chair. Listen carefully to these people, who just might see the situation more clearly than you do.

3. Sometimes an outside, objective evaluator can listen to the chief executive, board members, staff, and other moral owners and provide an analysis that helps answer the question of chief executive tenure.

4. Well in advance of a leadership crisis, work with the board to develop policies addressing succession planning, severance benefits, search and transition guidelines, and related issues.

48

How can a board facilitate the end of the employment relationship with its chief executive?

"Hiring and firing a chief executive are among the board's most important tasks."

If hiring and firing the chief executive are not the most important tasks of the board, they surely rank right up there with mission, policies, and financial viability. Let's look at some ways to handle the matter. The board can manage the chief executive's termination in a variety of ways: by encouraging retirement, by prompting him or her to begin a job search, by requesting his or her resignation, or by firing. How the board manages the loss of a key player in each of these situations will affect the whole organization. It is vital for the board to exercise care, forthrightness, grace, and sensitivity to the needs of the person and the organization.

Naturally, the full board must support a decision to terminate employment of the chief executive. Although the executive committee frequently conducts performance and compensation reviews on behalf of the board, the full board should be involved in any transitions of the one staff member who reports to them. An executive session at the end of every board meeting provides the opportunity for anyone to ask whether it is time for a new chief executive.

RETIREMENT

When a long-standing chief executive reaches age 60 or so, he or she is probably wondering about the best time to retire. An alert board is probably thinking about the same thing. More often than not, the answer is a result of honest conversations between the chief executive and the board chair and perhaps other board members. It is common for a board, perhaps during the chief executive's annual evaluation, to suggest retirement. Many factors may feed this conclusion: an upcoming capital campaign, a merger, a move to a different city, the planned retirement of a 20-year chief program officer or chief financial officer. Whatever the reason, some boards have the option of encouraging retirement sooner rather than later.

To encourage a somewhat reluctant chief executive, the board might offer a one-year sabbatical prior to retirement, or perhaps the title "emeritus" along with a year of half-time paid work on special projects. The point is to honor a chief executive who has given several good years and, at the same time, to move the organization toward new staff leadership.

JOB CHANGE

It may be best for the chief executive to announce his or her departure to take another job. But it may take a lunch with the board chair to prompt the chief executive to start looking. This approach to terminating a chief executive is appropriate when there is no urgency in making a change, when the chief executive has many loyal supporters who would be upset if the person were fired, and when the board thinks an insider should be groomed over several months to step in.

235

How can a board facilitate the end of the employment relationship with its chief executive?

If this saving-face maneuver seems too time consuming and an immediate transition is appropriate, the board may need to think about the next alternative.

FORCED RESIGNATION

An emotional whirlwind usually accompanies a chief executive's sudden announcement that he or she is leaving at the end of the month. It happens in many ways, but essentially the board has decided that some action or inaction requires a fairly quick exit on the part of the executive. This is never easy and seldom a pleasant way to fulfill the board's responsibility to the organization's stakeholders. The local media or the organization's newsletter often will explain that there are "personal reasons" for the departure. Most people will know this tactic is just a nice spin on being fired, but it is a good option that protects the organization from negative press and leaves some dignity to the chief executive and his or her family.

Perhaps the board has put off dealing with unpleasant issues for some time and finally decides to take action. The chair is again asked to deliver a blunt message: "For these reasons, the board wants to give you the option of resigning at the end of this month or being fired on Friday." Most chief executives would prefer to resign and have some influence over how the announcement is made.

If the situation leading up to the termination has potential legal ramifications, often an attorney will be asked to draft a memorandum of understanding that spells out what the board or the chief executive can say in public about the situation. If this painful and sensitive process is not best, the last option may be necessary.

TERMINATION

When a chief executive is fired, he or she often has made decisions or statements that have riled the public — or at least enough donors and supporters to create a crisis. Staff may be threatening to leave. A foundation may want to pull back on its funding. An aggrieved employee may have gone public with some indiscretion on the part of the chief executive. Whatever the reason, for the integrity and progress of the organization, the board realizes that everyone is looking to them to act. The only reasonable thing to do is exercise good trusteeship and terminate the chief executive.

Firing the chief executive is one of the least pleasant things a board can do. The board must ensure that such action never comes as a surprise to the chief executive. The entire board should agree on the action after a board meeting or conference call. There should be good documentation of the performance or lack of performance that led to the action. The chief executive should be told first, before anyone else. To reduce the possibility of costly legal battles, an attorney should be asked to draft a mutually agreeable document. The staff should be briefed on who will be the acting chief executive. A press release may be in order. The chair should send a letter to donors and special friends. A process should be put in place soon to find a replacement. In other words, the board leadership must think the whole thing through in advance, whether that means taking five hours or five days to do.

SUGGESTED ACTION STEPS

1. Establish regular board performance evaluations of the chief executive so the need for dramatic surprises is reduced.

2. Have a succession plan in place, or at least a predetermined process for conducting an executive search.

3. When a chief executive nears retirement age, encourage a good private conversation between the executive committee and the chief executive about the near-term future.

Part VI

The Board's Role in Financial Management

49

What is the board's role in monitoring an organization's finances?

*"As a board, we talk about money all the time,
but I don't understand most of it."*

Staying on top of financial issues without being consumed by them is a big challenge for many boards. If board members must know one thing, it is their responsibility for helping the organization to stay financially viable with integrity.

The level of financial detail board members receive can be confusing to the layperson. For this reason, many boards try to have a few members who understand the intricacies of budgets, investments, audits, and financial reporting. These board members typically are assigned to the finance committee. But the rest of the board must also take finances seriously. Boards should organize this important task so policies, budgets, and financial reports are clear and concise, allowing board members to fulfill their other functions more easily.

Every board member has the responsibility to participate in these four areas:

POLICIES

Every board should have organized, written financial policies that spell out its desires regarding matters such as controls on cash receipts and disbursements, budget practices, investments, operating reserves, capital budgets, risk management, financial reports, and audits. These policies can be written in language everyone understands. They guide the staff and enable the board to be as involved as they should be.

BUDGET

Some argue that the budget is a management tool, not a governance tool and that sound board policies on finance make budget approval unnecessary. In reality, even with good policies in place, most nonprofit boards like to see and approve the annual budget. Budget discussions often bring out critical assumptions and policy matters that might be overlooked. The budget serves as a useful reference for financial reports. However, the level of detail in the board-approved budget should be less than what the chief executive and chief financial officer need. Revenues and expenditures can shift frequently throughout the year, so budget policies should define the staff's flexibility to move funds within or between budget categories.

FINANCIAL REPORTS

The board should understand the various financial statements nonprofits use, then state in board policies what reports it wants and when it wants them. The typical reports are statements of financial position, statements of financial activities, and statements of cash flow. Tabular reports should be supplemented with graphics, trend data, comparison data with similar organizations, and adequate commentary to highlight important budget variances and other important points.

241

What is the board's role in monitoring an organization's finances?

GOOD QUESTIONS

It doesn't take a financial expert to ask good questions. Often, board discussion about the financial reports forces additions to policies, suggests new ways to present the budget, or prompts new reports. Questions might include:

- Do we have adequate reserves should our government funding end next year?

- Do we actually put money in the budget for the required depreciation expenses in case we need a new roof?

- What percentage of our total expenditures goes for staff compensation, and how does that compare with our competitors?

- Would the revenue from our potential business partnership require us to pay unrelated business income taxes?

A good question can ward off potential problems before they arise.

The chief executive should synthesize all financial details into periodic board reports. Effective boards receive brief summaries along with more detailed information for finance committee members and others who wish to digest more. A monthly statement from the chief executive might say "We are 10 percent over budgeted revenues and 6 percent under budgeted expenditures. With donor income about the same as the last three years at this point, we project ending the year with $40,000 to $50,000 more in net reserves than planned. It is a good year financially." This short report can be accompanied by seven pages of financial reports, the last budget, and the most recent audit. Although only a few people may delve into all the details, good stewardship and good governance require that all board members have access to complete information about the organization's financial status.

SUGGESTED ACTION STEPS

1. Give each board member a blank index card and ask this question: "On a scale of 1 to 10, how satisfied are you that you understand our finances to the extent you feel you should?"

2. Ask a CPA or auditor who works with nonprofit organizations to make a board presentation on this topic.

3. If you do not have written board policies to guide the staff in all areas of finance, discuss who should work with the chief executive and the chief financial officer to draft them.

How do boards ensure long-term financial viability?

"We've never had a year where we didn't scramble to break even."

The road to long-term financial viability is different for every organization. Reaching this goal depends on the type and age of the organization, its values, the nature of the competition, leadership, and much more. Some nonprofits are successful risk takers. Others are conservative in approach and slowly add to their net reserves each year. In education and the arts, endowments are well accepted. In some other organizations, endowments may not be tolerated.

Effective boards score high on the basics: clear mission, reasonable yet forward-looking goals, the right mix of board members, written policies that give significant freedom to professional staff, loyal donors, multiple sources of revenue, and wise use of available funds. These elements are among the most critical:

- *Clear, well-communicated mission and goals.* No one wants to give money to organizations whose purpose is unclear or whose successes are not well known.

- *Financial discipline.* More and more major donors want to know some details about policies, monitoring reports, and financial controls.

- *Reserves.* Every nonprofit should build up a rainy-day fund to cushion unexpected shifts in the economy, dramatic changes in donations, loss of a major revenue source, and cycles of heavy spending within each fiscal year. Depending on mission, financial philosophy, and donors' attitudes, the board should set a goal for the amount of unrestricted reserves that can be justified.

- *Multiple revenue sources.* As in a personal investment portfolio or a regional economy, depending on one or two revenue sources can result in a crisis when even one source dries up.

Let's focus on multiple revenue sources. How many of the more than 30 possible ways to generate income listed in Figure 10 does your organization tap? Creativity and alliances with other organizations are necessary for most nonprofit corporations today. Some of the options in this chart require business partnerships, risk taking, and legal and tax challenges, but others could be natural, low-risk extensions of what you are already doing.

The challenge is to match the mission to the money. While some boards think membership dues will always amount to 90 percent of revenues, a membership base creates all kinds of opportunities for providing a service and generating new revenue streams at the same time. Some charities have always depended on mail solicitation, but major donor giving—including deferred giving through a planned giving program—makes mass mailings a poor strategy for organizations whose mission is directed toward a small group of people or organizations. Many nonprofits are finding entrepreneurial ways to generate enough earned income that contributed income becomes a pool of extra money for special projects.

Boards who achieve and maintain long-term financial viability obviously do many things well, including hiring and retaining top staff. Visionary staff can take an organization into activities that might create new revenues. But these activities may also confuse stakeholders and make the organization vulnerable to external variables over which it has no control. Boards find it hard to say no to new revenue sources, but often that is the best long-term decision. Sticking to the mission and major goals helps both board and staff resist chasing ideas just for the money.

Long-term financial viability is less of a strategy than the outcome of hundreds of good practices and wise decisions over time. There are many means to achieve that end. But it is not the most important end. Achieving your mission has that spot locked up.

246

NONPROFIT BOARD ANSWER BOOK

Figure 10

POTENTIAL SOURCES OF INCOME FOR NONPROFIT ORGANIZATIONS

Revenues and Reimbursements

Memberships

Tuition and registration fees

Contracts

Sales

Subscriptions

Insurance and other reimbursements

Interest income on investments

Fees for services

Other

Contributions and Grants

	Individuals	Government	Business	Foundations	Nonprofit Organizations
	(Current and deferred giving)				
Annual giving	√		√		√
Mass appeal	√				
Program or operational grants	√	√	√	√	√
Events	√		√		
Capital funds	√		√	√	√
In-kind	√		√		√

Investment Income

	Organization	For-Profit Subsidiary
Cash and fixed income accounts	√	
Securities	√	
Real estate rental	√	
Real estate development/sales	√	
Dividends from subsidiary		√
Sale of subsidiary		√
Other?	√	√

Source: The ideas for these categories were stimulated by Fisher Howe, *The Board Member's Guide to Fund Raising* (San Francisco, CA: Jossey-Bass Publishers, 1991).

SUGGESTED ACTION STEPS

1. Develop a useful chart showing the sources of revenue for your organization over the past 10 years to see how sources might have shifted.

2. Use the chart in this chapter (see Figure 10) to identify all the possibilities your board thinks are worthy of more study.

3. Create some benchmarks to measure your financial strength, including ratios that reflect good practices in similar organizations.

51

What is the board's role in the annual financial audit?

"I know we have an audit, but I don't know anything beyond that."

We all know that an annual external financial audit by a competent firm is good practice. But in fact, the board should be more involved in the audit — and get a better product — than typically is the case.

Many factors heighten the importance of external audits. Since 1996, the IRS has had the authority to impose intermediate sanctions (fines) for improper inside transactions; this authority has replaced the more distant threat of revoking an organization's exempt status. Watchdog agencies are more active and have access to more information. Donors increasingly want evidence of sound financial practices. And the media seem to enjoy finding irregularities that embarrass the nonprofit sector. Boards have their own concerns, especially fulfilling their fiduciary responsibilities when accounting standards, federal, state, and local laws, IRS regulations, and government grant restrictions keep changing. How can a board member ever know enough about these financial intricacies?

Fund accounting is far different from what most business people are used to, so an external audit is the best way for board members to be assured that the organization's financial systems and safeguards are appropriate.

What if an organization cannot afford a full audit or believes its finances are too limited to justify one? One option for a small nonprofit is to conduct an audit every two or three years. At a minimum, the board should ask an independent certified public accountant to review the staff's accounting and reporting procedures. To fulfill the board's fiduciary responsibility to the public, some external oversight is almost essential.

How can the board and staff get the most benefit from an audit firm? Here is a checklist:

1. Delegate responsibility to a committee.

An audit committee or task force should have responsibility for the range of activities linked to an audit. The committee should include a few people who are familiar with finance and accounting. While staff work most closely with the auditor, the board must assume responsibility for defining the scope of work and for leading the implementation of the audit and the suggestions included in the management letter.

2. Outline expectations.

Working with the chief financial officer, the committee should describe its expectations beyond what most firms would do in the course of a typical audit. It may be important to evaluate the accounting practices of your international sites, or perhaps you want to focus on how accounts payable are handled. The basic audit package will include internal accounting practices, controls, financial management, and financial reports. If requested, some firms will also prepare the IRS Form 990.

3. Solicit proposals.

The committee should then ask for proposals from two or three audit firms with experience in the nonprofit sector. Better yet, look for firms that have audited similar organizations or have proven experience with your particular needs. While there are advantages to working with the same firm each year, it's wise to change audit firms periodically to ensure objectivity.

4. Review the proposals, conduct interviews, and recommend a firm.

This step will give the committee confidence in the firm it recommends to the board. Audit costs can vary from a few thousand dollars to tens of thousands, depending on the size and complexity of the organization's financial structure, so the value received is an important question.

5. Conduct the audit.

Staff usually assist with the audit, which begins shortly after the end of the fiscal year, as soon as the records are organized. One or two accountants typically visit the site to examine financial records and interview staff. The board is unlikely to be involved at this stage.

6. Review a draft report and management letter.

If possible, the audit firm should prepare a draft report and management letter for the chief financial officer and staff. This review often prompts new questions or signals to the audit firm that they overlooked something important. The chief financial officer may be asked to provide a written response to the draft.

7. Distribute the final audit report to the audit or finance committee.

The committee should read the audit report and management letter carefully and invite the auditors to discuss their findings. This is the time to ask the auditors about any special concerns and to understand any recommendations, often contained in a separate management letter. It's wise to afford the board or audit committee time to review the audit alone with the auditors. This allows the board the comfort to ask questions that might be delicate in front of staff. The audit committee acts on behalf of the board and keeps the board apprised of its concerns and recommendations.

The board's fiduciary role has other elements besides the external audit, including a review of the following:

- Insurance policies as part of its risk management oversight
- Pending lawsuits or audits required by the government or other funders
- Finance staff assignments, technology, internal controls
- Inventory schedules
- Investment policies
- Conflict of interest policy

Some boards take their fiduciary responsibilities to extremes, from total dependence on the external audit to constant micromanaging. It is important to seek a balance, even when staff reporting is comprehensive and tempts the board into neglecting this important function. Staff should welcome rather than resist a board's interest in doing its audit functions well.

SUGGESTED ACTION STEPS

1. If you do not engage an independent audit firm every year or every other year, ask a few board members to investigate your options and report back.

2. Add value to your audit firm's services by asking the assigned board committee to brainstorm with staff about the specific issues next year's audit should include.

3. Help the board assume responsibility for monitoring other aspects of the organization's financial activities.

Part VII

Other Critical Issues

52

When should a board enter into strategic alliances with other organizations?

"We just need more money to do all the things we want to do."

Strategic alliances can provide the essential leverage that helps nonprofit organizations fulfill their missions and expand the range of people they serve. Few organizations can do it all. Fewer still can afford it all. And one plus one can often equal three in the nonprofit world. These alliances can take a variety of forms: public-private partnerships, joint initiatives with organizations with similar missions, partnerships with community groups that reflect your actual or potential constituents, or contractual agreements with organizations that can help you deliver a service.

Consider this example. A young visionary in the midwest, Rick Little, had secured foundation grants to develop one of the best drug abuse prevention curriculums for schools. He engaged top scholars and the best design people, hired superb trainers to prepare school teachers, did the right pilot tests, and generally had a big winner. But how could this small, emerging organization market its product? Direct mail? Field salespeople? Telemarketing? The curriculum cost several hundred dollars, and the organization, wanting to ensure results, required schools to send teachers to training workshops. That is a hard sell: asking 15,000 school districts to pay more than modest sums to send their teachers to be trained by an unknown organization.

In keeping with its mission-driven nature, this group sought a relationship with an organization that would complement its assets. It formed a strong alliance with Lions Clubs International, one of the world's largest service organizations, which adopted drug-abuse prevention as a worldwide priority. This partner organization had an army of local members who could say to school superintendents and principals, "We believe our schools need this drug-abuse program, and we are willing to pay the cost if you adopt it and select the teachers to be trained."

A quality product was merged with the best sales force one could imagine. The result was rapid growth in the United States and in other countries, endorsements from major education organizations, large foundation grants, and a basis for more alliances.

Nonprofit organizations are reaching out in this way to other groups in the independent sector, to businesses, to media corporations, and to government agencies. In the corporate world, buying, selling, merging, joint-venturing, subcontracting, and outsourcing are common practices because they increase profits. Shouldn't nonprofits be doing more to improve their "bottom line" — providing services that change the quality of life for as many people as possible?

Nonprofits need leaders who can form strategic alliances. Harvard Business School professor Rosabeth Moss Kanter describes the "cosmopolitan" leader who has the "vision, skills, and resources to form networks that extend beyond their home base and to bring benefits to their own group by partnering with others." Cosmopolitan leaders, Kanter says,

must be integrators who can look beyond obvious differences
among organizations, sectors, disciplines, functions, or
cultures. They must be diplomats who can resolve conflicts
between the different ways that organizations or communities
or countries operate and who can influence people to work
together, to find common cause. They must be cross-fertilizers
who can bring the best from one place to another. And they
must be deep thinkers who are smart enough to see new
possibilities and to conceptualize them.[1]

Strategic alliances have such growing importance in the nonprofit world
that we hope every board will seek a chief executive who has these qualities
to pursue them. This type of leader can also influence an organization as a
board member, if the chief executive is willing to share in the vision casting.

The first step is to recognize the potential for fulfilling your mission
through partnerships and cooperation. Board and staff leaders must ask
these critical questions: What are our greatest assets? With whom could we
work to leverage them on behalf of more people? Which organizations
might want to forge strategic alliances with us? The next step is to encourage
board members, staff, volunteers, and donors to think strategically. Create
task forces to explore the possibilities. Consult a variety of sources to find
out what other organizations like yours are doing. Look for opportunities
where one plus one can equal three.

In pursuing strategic alliances, nonprofit organizations must be open to
fairly radical departures from the status quo. This kind of change
threatens many, including board members. The organization's mission,
corporate culture, leadership style, support constituencies, and much
more must be considered.

Among the criteria needed to evaluate potential collaboration are:

- Will it further our own mission?

- Do we and the proposed partner(s) have adequate staff and
  financial resources?

- Does it meet Internal Revenue Service and legal requirements?

- Is it the best way to achieve the desired results?

- Are the added work and coordination time worth it?

We believe there are many options that could meet these criteria, even if the alliance is as simple as splitting the salary of a shared staff member, the cost of a piece of equipment, or the use of a conference room. Collaboration does not need to be complex. Here are some additional guidelines to prompt your thinking:

1. The chief executive should lead in reaching out to other organizations, but within parameters set by the board.

2. Begin with an agreement to explore only those ideas that are win-win for the potential participating organizations.

3. When draft ideas are on paper, circulate them as widely as possible, and invite feedback.

4. Keep rewriting drafts until the best ideas are tested by enough people and a consensus emerges.

5. Invite a consultant to help in the final stages, especially in negotiating the financial aspects of the alliance.

6. Agree to a pilot period, after which any organization is free to pull out with proper notice.

7. Set realistic goals and agree up front on criteria for measuring success.

8. Remain open to including new partner organizations as long as everyone benefits.

9. Seek foundation grants for seed money; foundations like to see collaboration.

10. Be clear in advance about expectations. Define roles and responsibilities clearly.

11. Remember that authentic partnership results when there is a true need for the service you want to provide and when real benefits accrue to all parties.

12. Be willing to share the credit with other partners.

A commitment to pursue strategic alliances that further your organization's mission is a good posture for these times. But collaboration is another means of achieving your desired goals, not an end in itself. We believe so much in collaboration that we wish more foundations would say to applicants, "Don't send us any more grant requests unless they include at least one other organization besides yours." We hope you agree.

SUGGESTED ACTION STEPS

1. Ask your board and staff leaders whether your organization could benefit from strategic alliances that further its mission.

2. Ask eight to 10 volunteers who know your organization but have no vested interest in it to brainstorm and come up with 10 good ideas for strategic alliances. Take the list to the board for some "what if. . . ?" discussion.

3. Interview staff or board members from organizations that have entered into the kind of alliances you are considering. What have they learned?

---

1. Rosabeth Moss Kanter, "World-Class Leaders: The Power of Partnering," in *The Leader of the Future: New Visions, Strategies, and Practices for the Next Era,* ed. Frances Hesselbein, Marshall Goldsmith, and Richard Beckhard (San Francisco, CA: Jossey-Bass, 1996), p. 91.

53

When should a board hire a consultant or find a mentor?

*"We really need some expert, objective
help to get us back on track."*

Most organizational leaders need a consultant or mentor from time to time in some aspect of their jobs. Having served hundreds of nonprofit leaders in these capacities, we thought we would share some of our experience.

USING A CONSULTANT

Interest in nonprofit governance and leadership has increased dramatically in the last decade. Research and publications have expanded, and educational opportunities are widely available. Media coverage and foundation stimulus are among the other factors behind this growing interest. As a result, there are more lawyers, accountants, consultants, and other professionals who make a living by specializing in the independent sector.

Qualified consultants bring these benefits to an organization:

- experience gained from working with numerous other nonprofits;
- skill in group development, conflict resolution, and change management;
- objectivity with no vested interests;
- the discipline to focus on critical areas within your time frame;
- a network of resources that meet your needs; and
- information and ideas that help you long after the consultation is completed.

Even if board members or staff could do the task as well, the politics of some situations, or the lack of time to focus on the task, suggest the need for one or more consultants. Nonprofit clients use consultants to help them achieve important goals, including

- a national or international executive search;
- a comprehensive fund-raising program or a specialized campaign;
- preventive legal services, legal audits, and legal defense;
- accounting systems, financial audits, and investment strategy;
- technology planning and implementation;
- board development;
- organizational development and management training;
- public relations, publications planning, publications design, writing and editing; and
- large meeting planning.

The list could be much longer, as the increasing competition for funds and volunteers makes nonprofit organizations strive for greater professionalism. In addition, using a consultant for key tasks may be less expensive than hiring staff in a specialized area that does not require full-time effort.

Before you pay the typically higher consultants' fees, consider how two or three organizations could share the cost of a professional if none of them needs or can afford that kind of expertise full-time. For example, organizations need someone to set up internal computer networks, select software, position them on the World Wide Web, and train staff. Why not contract with a consultant full time, share the costs with a few other organizations, and each gain a pro rata share of the consultant's services? This approach can also work with development consultants, writers, lawyers, and others.

Here are some tips for finding and retaining a consultant:

- *Word of mouth is often the best source.* Call state or national associations. Look in their journals for articles written by consultants. Try to find people who have worked with similar organizations on similar projects.

- *Ask two or three potential consultants for client references.* Call them. Ask tough questions. Look for the right fit.

- *Discuss fees up front.* Most consultants are somewhat flexible on whether they will do an assignment on an hourly, daily, or fixed-fee basis. Be clear about travel time, out-of-pocket expenses, and payment schedule.

- *Put your agreement in writing.* Define specific expectations, outcomes, and deadlines. Be explicit about to whom the consultant is accountable — the chief executive, board chair, or someone else. Include conditions for altering or terminating the written agreement.

- *Keep communications open.* Do not hesitate to give a consultant direct feedback. He or she wants a successful relationship as much as you do.

USING A MENTOR

Sometimes what a chief executive or board chair needs is an outside expert who is available simply as a mentor. Although consultants sometimes do mentoring, you should not try to take advantage of someone just because you don't want to spend the money.

Good mentors are usually experienced, trusted colleagues who can offer advice, ideas, and objective feedback and who have the desire for meaningful volunteer work. Retired nonprofit executives and people who have served on a number of nonprofit boards are excellent possibilities. There are good books on mentoring, and many definitions of mentoring.[1] We mainly want to remind you that an independent, wise counselor is worth a great deal.

Some thoughts on starting a mentoring relationship:

- *Think of people you admire a great deal.* They may have good business sense, unusual vision, special skills relevant to your situation, or a network you would like to tap. Make a short list. Think about exactly what you would like from these people in a mentor relationship. Write it all down.

- *Invite one of these people to lunch.* Have in mind the mentoring arrangement you think would work best: weekly or monthly lunches, periodic phone calls, feedback on documents. Decide on a time frame. Then simply ask, "Would you be willing to be a mentor on this, maybe getting together every other week?" Most people are honored to be asked. If you share your vision and needs, most will respond positively if they can find the time. Besides, mentors often learn as much as the one they mentor.

- *Honor the commitment.* Provide helpful information. Be clear on the topics for discussion. Admit your vulnerabilities. Maintain confidentiality. Show appreciation. Pick up the lunch tab!

Sometimes the entire board benefits from having a mentor. Invite a savvy person experienced in board service to sit in on three or four meetings. Ask him or her to give honest feedback, sometimes to the entire board, sometimes to the board chair or chief executive. It is always amazing what an outside friend can see and hear that others seem to ignore.

✓

SUGGESTED ACTION STEPS

1. If you are the chief executive, ask your staff colleagues and friends where you personally could use some expert help. Consider with your board chair whether you should look for a consultant or mentor to help sharpen your weak areas.

2. If you are the board chair, ask whether you or the full board could benefit from outside counsel. Think in terms of the value received in light of your mission and total budget. Would you spend one percent of your budget to gain a 10 to 20 percent improvement in your governance or programs?

3. Think whether you could be someone else's mentor. Take the initiative. You will learn a lot yourself and make a difference in someone's life.

---

1. Ted W. Engstrom, with Norman B. Rohrer, *The Fine Art of Mentoring* (Brentwood, TN: Wolgemuth and Hyatt, 1989); Bobb Biehl, *Mentoring: Confidence in Finding a Mentor and Becoming One* (Nashville, TN: Broadman and Holman, 1996).

54

How should a board select
an advisory group?

*"I think our organization needs more credibility
and visibility in our region."*

In the last two chapters we discussed the value of looking outside the organization for assistance. Advisory groups, by whatever title, are another resource. When an ongoing advisory group lacks clear definition, however, the experience is frustrating and the potential benefits are lost.

The first step is to think through whether or not one or more advisory groups would help you achieve your mission. On the positive side, these groups can raise your credibility and visibility if properly handled. They can bring special expertise to your leadership. They bring new contacts and networks. Sometimes they bring new contributions. On the flip side, advisory groups require a time commitment that may not be worth it. Some advisory group members may not be seen by all as a positive association for your organization. And some strong advisory group members may try to compete with your board in setting policy. Are these latter risks worth it?

We think so. But move ahead thoughtfully. Here are some suggestions to help:

- *Set guidelines for creating advisory groups.* Both board and staff should have the authority to create advisory groups. But one group or person should not impose an advisory mechanism on another. The board has the prerogative to set parameters for advisory groups, such as approving their budgets. The board itself may decide to name one or more formal advisory groups, particularly to help them link to a larger, more diverse constituency. Other possibilities include a board alumni council, which we describe in Chapter 29. Or perhaps a small group of financial experts could advise the board on its endowment investment policies. Another group of people who are knowledgable about programs might help the board monitor and evaluate program results.

- *Choose an appropriate name.* Names including "board" or "committee" lead constituents to confuse advisory groups with the governing board and its committees. An exception might be a "board of reference," well-known advisors who agree to let their names be used by the organization. We also like the term "task force" for a group that is formed to complete a specific task and then terminated. An advisory "council" suggests an ongoing entity.

- *Describe the group's role.* Create a written description of each advisory group's purposes and accountability. Clarify that the group does not make final decisions for the organization; it is advisory. In fact, some argue that advisory groups should be "councils" focusing on specific topics. They never meet as a whole, but they are willing to be called upon individually or in small groups for specific purposes at different times. The point is to be clear about roles and responsibilities from the start.

- *Establish terms of service.* Do you know how hard it is to fire a volunteer who enjoys either the honor or the work of serving on a respected advisory council? You might want some people to stay on for a decade or more. But the advisory group member who gets media coverage about a questionable business deal is one you may want to ask to leave the group immediately, or at least you won't want to renew his or her term. Volunteers also like to know what they are getting into when they agree to these commitments. We like one-year renewable terms. Thank everyone at the end of the year, and invite some to continue. The composition of the group should be your choice.

- *Provide for formal leadership.* Volunteers often respond better when one of their own chairs an advisory group. This additional leadership role is often substantively and politically helpful to the board chair or the chief executive.

- *Plan for staff assistance.* Advisory groups add work for staff, and you should consider the additional cost before establishing them. Like board committees, they often need a staff liaison. The chief executive should select this person, or name himself or herself, to work alongside an advisory group. In addition to serving as a resource, the staff liaison also makes sure the group gets help in planning meetings and distributing background material.

- *Budget for expenses.* The organization should be ready to pay all out-of-pocket expenses for attending advisory group meetings. In some organizations, this is a sizable budget item. Although you should offer to reimburse everyone, some will choose not to submit vouchers. All unreimbursed expenses related to volunteer service for a 501(c)(3) corporation are tax deductible and you should inform advisory group members of these IRS regulations.

- *Provide appropriate publicity.* To be honest, many advisory groups are formed to give constituents, donors and potential donors, foundations, and other organizations more confidence in your organization. Giving public recognition to these good people and their efforts is certainly acceptable. But we have all seen organizations that publicize the big names of advisory group members, and we wonder whether those people would even remember agreeing to serve. Don't publicize more than is deserved.

Advisory groups are worth some thought. Every organization needs wise counsel, and an advisory group is another way of helping you be as effective as possible. Besides, if your vision and mission are relevant to society's needs, many sharp people are able and willing to contribute to your efforts.[1]

SUGGESTED ACTION STEPS

1. Interview the chief executives of five organizations that you know have advisory groups. Summarize their experience for your board.

2. Brainstorm with the board for 10 minutes on areas within the organization — board or staff — where outside advice might be used effectively.

3. Terminate an advisory group that no longer serves a purpose.

---

1. Nancy R. Axelrod, *The Advisory Committee* (Washington, DC: National Center for Nonprofit Boards [now BoardSource], 1998).

(55)

Why do board members
fail to act decisively?

*"It's amazing! Seventeen bright people know
the problem but can't vote to resolve it."*

We aren't psychologists or trained experts in organizational dynamics. But we see the frustration reflected in this question all the time. Be assured, if you see this happening continually on your board, it is not unusual.

An attempt to understand and alleviate board inaction might start with the selection of board members. William G. Bowen, who looks pragmatically at both corporate and nonprofit boards, observes: "Courage and the will to act are often the attributes in scarcest supply."[1] It is not enough to be knowledgeable, interested, well intentioned, and a willing donor. A board member must be ready and willing to make difficult value choices in a timely way and in public view of friends who might disagree. This attribute can be evaluated in advance. Make this one of your questions in doing reference checks on potential board members. And discuss this attribute with your prospects, explaining its importance to good governance.

The next barrier to clear, decisive policymaking is fuzzy role definitions. When some board members believe an issue is actually in the chief executive's domain, they are reluctant to let the board make the decision. After all, many argue, the staff knows so much more about most issues than board members do. The chief executive can often help in these situations by saying, "I really feel this is a board decision, and I am willing to implement whatever you decide." If the chief executive has a specific position, that should be stated, too, but always in the spirit of being willing to lead within the board's policies.

It helps the board to have policies, for example, that state the board should adopt a conflict-of-interest policy, an investment policy, a staff compensation policy, and other policies. Then it is clear what tasks the board is expected to accomplish. We have addressed some additional roles and responsibilities issues earlier. Adopting a standing board policies manual as a tool is a good way to anticipate major policy decisions, articulate board policy from the broad to the specific, and tell the chief executive to accept the board's approval to move ahead in achieving goals within the policy parameters.

Then there is the real experience of simply not knowing what is right, even when the facts are clear. In this case, an advisor, mentor, or advisory group might be able to help. Often, a neutral party can look at the same facts and make a good recommendation the board is willing to accept. This approach removes some of the uneasiness that boards sometimes feel in arriving at closure on controversial matters. Take conflict-of-interest policies. They come in all shapes and sizes, and sometimes put some board members on the defensive. An outside attorney or other knowledgeable person could come in to help the board settle on what is best for the group.

Last, but by no means least, we remind you that change is difficult for most people. Although a few people do thrive on change, especially when it does not affect their own well-being, most people in most groups will resist making decisions that will cause discomfort to others. Change, however, is what all of us can expect in greater doses and faster cycles. Boards must come to grips with an external world that is changing so fast that organizational decisions must be timely and relevant. This observation is especially true for organizations that might be in the mature or declining phase of their life cycles and desperately need renewal. In this case, a guest speaker or consultant could be briefed on the problems and asked to be forthright with the board.

For those of us who are change agents, indecisive boards can be very frustrating. Some board members resign if the problem persists. A healthier approach is to try different leverage points to improve the situation:

- Meet privately with the chair to see if he shares your frustration.

- Ask the board development committee to consider changes in the bylaws, board structure and process policies, or the board member profile grid defining desired characteristics of new board members that might help the board be more decisive.

- Suggest that the board invite a task force to look at a specific issue and report back to the board at the next meeting.

- Volunteer to work between meetings to come up with a recommendation that has been reviewed by the chief executive and a few board members.

- Put the issue on the agenda of the next board retreat.

- Get the board to set a deadline for resolving a particular issue, and encourage the chair to enforce that timetable for the good of the organization.

SUGGESTED ACTION STEPS

1. List the policies or policy areas that seem to get your board stuck.

2. Evaluate whether inaction is due to the board's leadership, the chief executive's posture, or something else.

3. As a board member, your last resort after trying to do what you feel is best is to resign without making such a big deal of it that it hurts the organization publicly.

---

1. Bowen, *Inside the Boardroom,* p. 48.

56

What conflict-of-interest policies should a board adopt?

*"Why don't we just buy all our vans from Jim?
He's been a good board member."*

Should the board and chief executive be concerned about conflict of interest? Absolutely. The integrity of the board and of the organization in the public's eyes is so important you must be conscious of both real and perceived conflicts of interest — or any other practice that casts doubt on the ethics of your organization. If you have questions about this topic after reading our chapter, we suggest you consult an attorney who is experienced in working with nonprofit organizations.

Usually, conflicts of interest happen innocently. Board members become friends. They trust one another. Staff respect their board members. It is natural to want to do business with someone you know and trust. Consider the following examples of nonprofits naively risking not just their good reputations but their tax-exempt status through questionable practices.

1. A large youth camp buys several vans and trucks. A board member owns a dealership and said he would give the camp a good deal. So the chief executive always goes to the board member for the purchases and service, never even thinking about the need to get bids to protect the board member from a conflict of interest for personal gain.

2. A board member for a mental health clinic has a daughter trying to start a desktop publishing business. He asks the chief executive to "contract with her, just for six months." The executive feels he has no choice because this is a good board member and a major donor. The result is a clear conflict of interest.

3. The chief executive of a popular literary society is a gifted writer. A publisher wanted to do a book, edited by the chief executive in his capacity as the organization's staff leader, and offered a nice advance. The chief executive used about 20 percent of his normal work week, while being paid his regular salary, to complete the task. He thought the book would be good public relations for his organization. He invested his advance and looked forward to royalties if the book sold well. This is staff conflict of interest, in our opinion, which should be regulated by a board policy on use of staff time and the organization's name for personal gain.

4. When the board of a community service organization decided it needed an attorney for considerable legal work, it naturally turned to John, the only attorney on the board and said, "You know us, so we hope you will do the work over the next year." The attorney accepted, billed the organization at his normal rate, and never once thought this was a conflict of interest.

Most conflicts of interest deal with money and other forms of personal gain. However, we feel that to have staff members other than the chief executive serving as voting members of the board is also a conflict of interest. Senior staff have too much at stake to be objective stewards of the organization at the governance level. While the practice is not illegal, watchdog and umbrella associations are recommending against these "inside" directors, a common practice in the corporate community.

Some board leaders we talk to, even when we point out a caution about potential conflicts, often reply, "We are all family here, and no one objects if we don't follow conflict of interest principles to the letter all the time." Those organizations are risking a lot. Board members must remember that the *unspoken* perceptions of other board members and staff affect morale, loyalty, and the pattern that staff accept as appropriate.

Every board needs a written policy that deals with actual and perceived conflicts of interest. This policy can be a few paragraphs or several pages.[1] It should explain matters such as board members absenting themselves from votes when there is a potential conflict, getting bids from several sources if a board member or family member are involved, and staff members using the organization's time and resources for personal gain. You might ask other organizations for copies of their policies, or consult your legal counsel. Please meet the legal requirements, the ethical standards of your national associations, and the highest moral standards members of your board choose to implement. You will never regret it. Take the high road, always.

SUGGESTED ACTION STEPS

1. Does your board have a written conflict-of-interest policy? If not, ask someone to research it, consult with legal counsel, and bring samples to the next meeting.

2. Set a goal of having a policy in place within four months, assigning responsibility for monitoring it, and reviewing it as a full board annually.

---

1. Daniel L. Kurtz, *Managing Conflicts of Interest: Practical Guidelines for Nonprofit Boards* (Washington, DC: National Center for Nonprofit Boards [now BoardSource], 2001).

57

What is a legal audit?

"As a board member, I'd like to have more confidence that we comply with the law."

A legal audit is a process of systematically reviewing all legal processes and documents, usually with professional help, to ensure that your legal risks are minimized. You should look into doing such an audit if you prefer prevention to crisis management.

Opting to have a legal audit conducted is a good voluntary decision on the part of the board or chief executive. It is time consuming, but not nearly as time consuming as defending a lawsuit or opposing IRS sanctions or a move to drop your exemption. With the average defense costs for even a civil suit running in the tens of thousands, a proactive legal audit is a bargain. This is another key component of best practices.

The reason for the increased popularity of legal audits is the changing legal and financial landscape for nonprofit organizations. Federal law, IRS regulations, state statutes, and court decisions in recent years have removed the traditional hands-off approach to nonprofits. Donors and employees have become more demanding and litigious at the same time. Many organizations are ticking time bombs because of lack of attention to the countless laws and changing regulations. A legal audit consists of the following steps:

1. Questionnaire

George R. Grange II, of Gammon & Grange, P.C., a McLean, Virginia, law firm specializing in nonprofits, explains that the starting point should be a comprehensive 100-page questionnaire that is filled out by employees. The questions provide a comprehensive checklist of the legal requirements an organization faces. A typical legal audit would include these broad categories, usually supplemented by other specific questions related to the mission of each organization:

- Governance
- Affiliate relationships
- Contractual relationships
- Financial operations and revenue strategies
- Financial books and written records
- Property
- Human resource management
- Exempt organization compliance
- Fund-raising
- Intellectual property
- Risk management and insurance
- International operations

Responding to the many questions may require from 50 to 100 hours of work on the part of staff. Grange's firm develops other, more focused, questions for senior management to address. Asking the right questions is key.

2. Document audit

Another component of many legal audits is the gathering and organizing of all documents relating to the topics above. This may be the first time several hundred pages of procedures, forms, board minutes, financial records, and other materials are found and organized.

3. Reports

Depending on the scope of the legal audit, the attorneys will report to the board and senior staff on their findings and recommendations. Sample procedures and templates for important documents are presented. This is the time to mention any specific concerns to the attorneys before they review the questionnaire.

An alternative to the questionnaire is to invite attorneys to do an on-site audit. With some gathering of materials in advance, this approach can save staff time and allow the attorneys to evaluate forms, contracts, and procedures while interacting with the responsible staff right on the spot. When taking this route, it is wise to think ahead of all the concerns and questions the board and staff have so the attorneys can focus on those. These visits can take one or more days, but it could be the best strategy in the long run.

Because a legal audit implies change, it deals with levels of detail many mission-driven executives neglect, and it requires a commitment of time and effort. Sadly, many organizations choose to believe no harm will come their way if their intentions are good. This could be a costly assumption. Preventive law is the way to go.

SUGGESTED ACTION STEPS

1. Show this chapter to the board officers and ask whether the board should be briefed on this useful approach to good practice.

2. Ask a good law firm that specializes in nonprofit organizations to send you information on their legal audit procedures and the approximate costs.

3. Ask yourself, "Would I sleep better if I knew we had gone through a legal audit and changed our procedures to comply with all laws and regulations that could put our organization at risk?"

(58)

When should a nonprofit organization consider closing up shop?

"How long can we hang on by our fingernails, anyway?"

Because many small (and some not-so-small) nonprofit organizations are facing closure, we want to comment briefly on this question. A board decision to shut down is not always bad news. The birth and death of organizations are parts of their life cycle.

Like small businesses in the for-profit world, most new nonprofits do not last beyond five years. Most had planned to, but circumstances led them to close. It is more newsworthy when a nonprofit organization that is 50 to 75 years old decides to shut its doors. Perhaps a few critical decisions here and there, an infusion of cash at the right time, or the arrival of a new leader who renews the enthusiasm of the moral owners could have held off the inevitable in some situations. But death is natural. There are always new visions and new energetic leaders ready to make their mark on society. After all, it takes only a few months and a few thousand dollars to gain nonprofit status from the government.

A board usually knows intuitively when it has moved from energy, growth, and vision to maintenance, defensiveness, and a sinking ship mentality. Then one or more board members should suggest looking at the options before they become no longer viable. Creativity, reaching out, taking initiative in opening a dialogue with other organizations' leaders — these are acts of leadership called for in such times.

It is most sad when the board or the chief executive sees the writing on the wall but chooses to ignore it or hopes that a miracle will change the trend line. We believe in miracles, but frankly we do not see many when it comes to organizations outliving their time. Even those whose faith carries them through hard periods tend to agree that there is a time to stop. If a board is open to this perspective, then it can monitor itself in an honest way and, at some point, decide to celebrate the good it has accomplished, pay off creditors, give staff ample notice, and leave with their heads held high.

If an organization does monitor itself carefully, it is possible to renew the vision and goals, change the direction of the downward curve, and begin another cycle of growth and energy. It takes courage and a positive, realistic philosophy to make this happen. Sometimes organizational renewal calls for drastic action — for example, the dismissal of a chair who has served for 20 years or the release of the visionary founder who cannot see the need to change. Whatever it takes, it may be worth keeping the name, constituency, staff, and programs in place.

Is your organization due for renewal? If participation rates, revenue, staff turnover, and other important indicators are heading in the wrong direction, renewal is one option. We don't think renewal happens by chance or in small increments. A "turnaround" situation calls for more drastic action, usually requiring a leadership change for board and staff and some intense time analyzing the external environment and rewriting the mission and major goals. These situations are not always the result of poor leadership. Often the world around the organization simply has changed faster than the organization. We caution, however, an organization attempting renewal should be very cautious about seeing borrowed money as the major way out of trouble.

MERGERS

Another positive option is a merger. In many cities and states, most knowledgeable observers would say there are too many nonprofit agencies trying to serve similar constituencies and draw from the same funding sources. A merger is not easy, but we feel many leaders will increasingly come to see that consolidating the strengths of two or three organizations into one is an act of great courage and foresight.[1] Mergers often get hung up on details, especially when the two organizations are not totally convinced a merger is best for both of them. We urge taking up to a year of regular talks, probably with a neutral facilitator, to put in writing the pros and cons of a merger, the costs, the shape of the board in the new organization, the roles of the two current chief executives, a proposed budget, and anything else that needs clarifying. Failure to agree on these points in advance can be a serious threat to the success of the new organization.

CLOSING THE DOORS

Sometimes the best option is closing the doors. While the organization is still healthy, it is wise for the board to agree on the signs that it should plan to shut down. These signs should be relevant to each organization, measurable, and both subjective and objective. Examples might include a minimum number of staff that can be supported, the depletion of reserve funds, or a drop in donors by more than 40 percent from the peak year. It helps to have concrete benchmarks, but people can often rationalize bad news as just a short-term problem. The real need is for a few respected board members to "stop the fight" just at the right time, while most people still have enough loyalty to thank one another for being part of past victories.

When the time for closing the door is imminent, bring in an attorney and a CPA to help the organization shut down its operations. It is also important to be honest with donors and beneficiaries, most of whom will honor the candor and try to help as the celebration of having done good begins. If the organization closes soon enough, there may be some funds left over after bills are paid and staff are given appropriate severance to pass along to a similar organization. The infusion of capital might allow that organization to continue serving some of your constituents or hire a few of your staff. Nonprofit hospitals that are sold to for-profit corporations actually end up with several million dollars to invest in another mission. But that situation is rare.

Some might feel that including this chapter near the end of the book is too negative. We feel just the opposite. Knowing when an organization should no longer exist is part of defining reality, as one of our friends has described the role of a leader.

SUGGESTED ACTION STEPS

1. If most board members agree your organization is faltering, schedule a board retreat or assign a task force to define what needs to be done to change the downward curve into a new phase of renewal.

2. If you are chair of an organization that might be on its last leg, quietly seek counsel in designing an honorable plan for closing the shop.

3. Assign someone to gather information on how and why organizations similar to yours terminated operations.

---

1. Thomas McLaughlin, *Seven Steps to a Successful Nonprofit Merger* (Washington, DC: National Center for Nonprofit Boards [now BoardSource], 1996); David LaPiana, *Nonprofit Mergers: The Board Member's Responsibility to Consider the Unthinkable* (Washington, DC: National Center for Nonprofit Boards [now BoardSource], 1994).

What is the best way to engage former chief executives and board members?

"Our retired chief executive refuses to stay out of our business, and that's a real problem."

Former nonprofit leaders would make fascinating case studies. There are examples of tremendous success, and there are horror stories that seem surreal. Let's look at both sides, starting with former chief executives.

Founding chief executives typically commit their lives to what they started. So when it comes to retirement, don't count on losing track of them. Their bodies may be weary at some point, but their commitment to see their vision fulfilled remains. It can be touchy. Some boards award an emeritus title. Others make the founder (or maybe another endeared chief executive) a member of the board. This practice is unwise, as logical as it might appear. The key is to be highly sensitive to the wishes of the current chief executive. If the new leader welcomes some continued involvement of one or more former chief executives, let him or her make that determination, not the board.

One of the best ways to engage former chief executives is to retain them part-time to continue relations with major donors. After all, some experts say it takes five years to nurture a person of wealth to make a major gift. But it usually does not work to have that person in the office much. And the past chief executive should always be accountable to the current one in terms of goals, working conditions, and compensation.

That said, in larger organizations the best wisdom for a departing chief executive is to keep a low profile and maintain a significant distance from the organization for at least a year. There are too many staff, board members, donors, clients, and others who will be tempted to run to the person they know, causing inevitable problems for the new leader.

Former board members are much easier to deal with. They typically are among the most knowledgeable and committed of all volunteers. The principle might be "Never lose a good volunteer." Here are some ways to engage them:

- *Recognition.* The most basic way to keep someone mentally and emotionally (and maybe financially) involved is to express appreciation at the end of his or her board service. A well-deserved plaque or other gift at the last board meeting is often the key to keeping a person engaged with the organization.

- *Board committees.* Term limits might force a board member to step down from the board for at least one year. If the person has been a good board member and you think the board would want to bring him or her back in a year or two, find a useful interim assignment. If the bylaws allow it, assign an interested former board member to a board committee.

- *Emeritus status.* Some boards decide to award emeritus status to a member who has a long and distinguished service record—but not to every former board member. An emeritus board member is generally considered to be a member for life, thereby negating any term limits or age restrictions. It is wise to clarify that the position is nonvoting

285

What is the best way to engage former chief executives and board members?

because the member's attendance is often too sporadic for committee assignments and meeting quorums.

- *Board alumni council.* Some boards create a special group only for former board members who served a minimum number of years. For example, after a total of 12 years of board service, a person is automatically a lifetime member of the board alumni council, with the right to attend future board meetings as an observer; some boards allow alumni to speak but not vote. The chief executive usually sends this group special mailings, highlights them in the newsletter or Web site, or provides other recognition. These friends of the organization also offer special fund-raising potential.

- *Special assignment.* Form a task force for a former board member to lead. Put him or her on an advisory group or assign a special study. Keep him or her challenged and engaged. If qualified, perhaps this person could be hired as a consultant to staff. The idea is never to lose the involvement of a talented and committed volunteer.

- *Mailings.* It should go without saying that loyal volunteers should be kept informed even after formal assignments are finished. Some chief executives continue to send board updates to former board members, often prompting a friendly idea by return mail. For sure, this practice generates good will.

In all of these examples, the idea is to honor good work and keep the communications channels open to these special people. We can never find enough ways to honor board members, whether during or after their active service.

In certain situations future involvement of board members may be desirable. When board members voluntarily resign or leave at the end of a first term expressing no desire to be re-elected, you are probably getting the signal that something has not worked well. Still, this assumption should be checked. Maybe the former board member simply wants to volunteer in a different way. Never let a former board member just drift into the dusk without a debriefing and a candid conversation about his or her desired level of continued involvement.

While expectations are high when a board member is first elected to the board, not all find it a good fit. Certainly this happens when the board has to terminate a noncontributing board member. Still, it is always best to make an early exit as civil and respectful as possible.

Finally, some former board members, particularly those in the same community as the staff headquarters, may need a gentle reminder that they need to let the current, active board members do the governing. This is true particularly in small organizations where the line between governing and volunteering was never clear. These "shadow" leaders may continue to interfere with the work of the board or staff because of their deep devotion to the mission. But they can also frustrate board and staff and need to be helped into a new and clearly defined volunteer role.

Is it possible that the same level of planning and caring that go into recruiting a new board member should be applied to a departing board member? Often, that is the case.

SUGGESTED ACTION STEPS

1. Ask the board development committee or a board task force to study how you relate to former board members.

2. Invite someone to interview former board members, in person or by phone, to gauge their feelings about their former status.

3. Brainstorm for 10 minutes during a board meeting how you might advance the mission more successfully by finding new ways to engage former board members.

Concluding thoughts

"I never dreamed there was so much to think about!"

We began this project together. We hoped to make this book more of a conversation with board leaders and chief executives in the trenches than an attempt at a textbook. We hope you have been stimulated by our perspectives, understanding that there are many good principles and practices — and some that are not so good, but used often — that might differ from ours. We simply hope to reduce the number of boards that are doing the wrong things better and better.

If you take anything from our experience, take the principle that boards and chief executives have different, noncompeting roles. They must learn to complement one another for each to be truly successful. Our friend Peter Drucker is good at getting to the essence of many things. Consider how he underscores this point:

> Nonprofits waste uncounted hours debating who is superior
> and who is subordinate —the board or the executive officer.
> The answer is that they must be colleagues. Each has a

different part, but together they share the play. Their tasks are complementary. Thus, each has to ask, "What do I owe the other?" not — as board and executive officers still tend to do — "What does the other owe me?"[1]

This is what servant-leadership is all about — each side of the dual leadership wanting the best for the other and taking initiative to help the other succeed. Everyone wins. Service in the organization is rewarding. Lives are changed for the better.

We are grateful beyond words that our career paths led us at early stages of life to give our best to the nonprofit sector. This community of more than one million mission-driven organizations has an ever-increasing role in our society. If you are in this sector — or even thinking about devoting more of your best to this sector — your choice will be honored.

This week, thousands of chief executives and board members of the nation's well over 700,000 charitable and religious nonprofit agencies will sit down together once again to do the work entrusted to them. Perhaps you will be one of them. May you be better prepared to carry out your assignments, to provide leadership for the people who look to you for direction, and to go the distance for your organization. Focus on the goal, aim to win, stay the course, and guard your heart.

Everything is possible in a team effort if it doesn't matter who gets the credit.

---

1. Peter Drucker, quoted in Richard P. Chait, Thomas P. Holland, and Barbara E. Taylor, *The Effective Board of Trustees* (Washington, DC: American Council on Education, 1993), p. 115.

Further Reading

Abbott, Langer & Associates. *Compensation in Nonprofit Organizations*. Crete, IL: Abbott, Langer & Associates, 2000.

Albert, Sheila. *Hiring the Chief Executive*. Washington, DC: National Center for Nonprofit Boards (now BoardSource), Revised 2000.

American Association of Fund-Raising Counsel. *Giving USA*. Indianapolis: AAFRC, 2001.

American Society of Association Executives. *Association Executives Compensation Study*. Washington, DC: ASAE, 2000.

Andringa, Robert C. *The Executive Committee: Making It Work for Your Organization*. Washington, DC: National Center for Nonprofit Boards (now BoardSource),1994.

Axelrod, Nancy R. *The Advisory Committee*. Washington, DC: National Center for Nonprofit Boards (now BoardSource), 1998.

Biehl, Bob. *Mentoring: Confidence in Finding a Mentor and Becoming One*. Nashville: Broadman and Holman, 1996.

Bobowick, Marla J., Sandra R. Hughes, and Berit M.Lakey. *Transforming Board Structure: Strategies for Committees and Task Forces*. Washington DC: National Center for Nonprofit Boards (now BoardSource), 2001.

Bowen, William G. *Inside the Boardroom: Governance by Directors and Trustees*. New York: John Wiley & Sons, 1994.

Bryson, John M. *Strategic Planning for Public and Nonprofit Organizations*. San Francisco: Jossey-Bass, 1988.

Carver, John. *Boards that Make a Difference*. 2nd ed. San Francisco: Jossey-Bass, 1997.

_____. *Reinventing Your Board*. San Francisco, CA: Jossey-Bass, 1997.

Chait, Richard P., Thomas P. Holland, and Barbara E. Taylor. *Improving the Performance of Governing Boards*. Phoenix: Oryx Press, 1996.

Dietel, William and Linda Dietel. *The Board Chair Handbook*. Washington, DC: National Center for Nonprofit Boards (now BoardSource), 2001.

Dingman, Robert W. *In Search of a Leader: The Complete Search Committee Guidebook*. Westlake Village, CA: Lakeside Books, 1989.

Draper, Lee. "A Dubious Legacy." *Foundation News & Commentary*, March/April 2001. Washington, DC: Foundation Center, 2001.

Eadie, Douglas. *Extraordinary Board Leadership: The Seven Keys to High-Impact Governance*. Gaithersburg, MD: Aspen Publishers, 2001.

Engstrom, Ted W., with Norman B. Rohrer. *The Fine Art of Mentoring*. Brentwood, TN: Wolgemuth and Hyatt, 1989.

Grange II, George "Chip" R. , Peter F. Rathbun, and Jonathan A. Ruybalid. "An Unfelt Need Whose Time Has Come." *Preventive Law Reporter*, Winter 1995.

Greenleaf, Robert K. *Servant Leadership: A Journey into the Nature of Legitimate Power and Greatness*. New York: Paulist Press, 1983.

Hadelman, Jordan M. "When You Have to Fire Your CEO. . . You Haven't Done Your Job" in *Trustee*, January 1996. Chicago: American Hospital Association, 1996.

Herman, Robert D. and Richard D. Heimovics. *Executive Leadership in Nonprofit Organizations: New Strategies for Shaping Executive-Board Dynamics*. San Francisco: Jossey-Bass, 1991.

Houle, Cyril O. *Governing Boards: Their Nature and Nurture*. San Francisco: Jossey-Bass, 1989.

Hughes, Sandra R., Berit M. Lakey, and Marla J. Bobowick. *The Board Building Cycle*. Washington, DC: National Center for Nonprofit Boards (now BoardSource), 2000.

Ingram, Richard T. *Ten Basic Responsibilities of Nonprofit Boards*, rev. ed. Washington, DC: National Center for Nonprofit Boards (now BoardSource), 1997.

Johnson, Sandra. *The Audit Committee*. Washington, DC: National Center for Nonprofit Boards (now BoardSource), 1994.

Kurtz, Daniel L. *Managing Conflicts of Interest: Practical Guidelines for Nonprofit Boards*. Washington, DC: National Center for Nonprofit Boards (now BoardSource), 2001.

Lang, Andrew S. *Checks & Balances*. Washington, DC: National Center for Nonprofit Boards (now BoardSource), 2001.

LaPiana, David. *Nonprofit Mergers: The Board Member's Responsibility to Consider the Unthinkable*. Washington, DC: National Center for Nonprofit Boards (now BoardSource), 1994.

McLaughlin, Thomas A. *Presenting: Nonprofit Financials: An Overview of Board Fiduciary Responsibility*. 60 slides, 12 page User's Guide. Washington, DC: National Center for Nonprofit Boards (now BoardSource), 2001.

McLaughlin, Thomas A. *Seven Steps to a Successful Nonprofit Merger*. Washington, DC: National Center for Nonprofit Boards (now BoardSource), 1996.

McManus, Joyce M., and Donald R. Leslie. "Resignation or Dismissal? When a CEO and a President Clash," in *Nonprofit Management & Leadership*, Winter 2000. San Francisco: Jossey Bass, 2000.

Moss Kanter, Rosabeth. "World-Class Leaders: The Power of Partnering," in *The Leader of the Future: New Visions, Strategies, and Practices for the Next Era*, ed. Frances Hesselbein, Marshall Goldsmith, and Richard Beckhard. San Francisco: Jossey-Bass, 1996.

National Center for Nonprofit Boards. "Brave New World: Bringing Technology into the Boardroom," in *Board Member*, V. 7, #8. Washington, DC: National Center for Nonprofit Boards (now BoardSource), 1998.

National Center for Nonprofit Boards. *The Board Meeting Rescue Kit*. Washington, DC. National Center for Nonprofit Boards (now BoardSource), 2001.

National Center for Nonprofit Boards. *Self-Assessment for Nonprofit Governing Boards*. Washington, DC: National Center for Nonprofit Boards (now BoardSource), 1999.

O'Connell, Brian. "Recruiting, Encouraging, and Evaluating the Chief Staff Officer," Chapter 8 in *The Board Member's Book*, 2nd ed. New York: Foundation Center, 1993.

Pierson, Jane and Joshua Mintz. *Assessment of the Chief Executive: A Tool for Boards and Chief Executives of Nonprofit Organizations*. Washington, DC: National Center for Nonprofit Boards (now BoardSource), 1995.

Reider, Rob. *Improving the Economy, Efficiency, and Effectiveness of Not-for-Profits: Conducting Operational Reviews*. New York, NY: John Wiley & Sons, 2001.

Robinson, Maureen. *Nonprofit Boards That Work: The End of One-Size-Fits-All Governance*. New York: John Wiley & Sons, 2001.

Robinson, Maureen. *Developing the Nonprofit Board*. Washington, DC: National Center for Nonprofit Boards (now BoardSource), 1994.

Robinson, Maureen. *The Chief Executive's Role in Developing the Board*. Washington, DC: National Center for Nonprofit Boards (now BoardSource), 1998.

Rutledge, Jennifer M. *Building Board Diversity*. Washington, DC: National Center for Nonprofit Boards (now BoardSource), 1994.

Saffold, Guy S. *Strategic Planning for Christian Organizations*. Fayetteville, AR: Accrediting Association of Bible Colleges, 1994.

Taylor, Barbara E., Richard P. Chait, and Thomas P. Holland. "The New Work of the Nonprofit Board," in *Harvard Business Review*, September/October 1996. Boulder, CO: Harvard Business Review, 1996.

Tranquada, Robert E. *The Compensation Committee*. Washington, DC: Association of Governing Boards of Colleges and Universities, 2001.

Vaughan, James S., and Catherine J. Robbins. "Best Financial Practices for Trustees." in *Trustee*, March 2001. Chicago: American Hospital Association, 2001.

Index

Building Board Diversity, 114
Bylaws
    board structure outline, 54
    changes, 72
    IRS requirement for exempt status, 198

C

Carver, John, 4, 20, 28, 71
Chairs. *See* Board chairs; Committee chairs
Chief executives
    appointment of, 216
    average tenure of, 227–228
    board-centered leadership, 219–222
    as board chair, 61
    board chair's support of, 64
    board improvement role, 218–222
    board member recruitment responsi-
    bilities, 100–102, 221
    characteristics of successful leaders, 190–196
    comparison of chief executive roles with
    board's roles, 19, 287–288
    compensation for, 207–211
    deciding to step down, 227–232
    designating two chief executives, 200–201
    differentiating from chief operating
    officers, 201
    engaging former chief executives, 283–286
    evaluation of, 202–206
    executive committee role, 59
    facilitating end of employment relation-
    ship with board, 233–236
    finding a new chief executive, 212–217
    forced resignations, 235
    functioning without a chief executive,
    197–201
    fund-raising role, 32
    identifying candidates, 214–215
    importance of, 198–200
    interviewing, 215
    job changes, 234–235
    leadership styles, 191–196, 219
    as members of the board, 183–185, 220
    negotiations with, 216
    no-vote policy, 184–185, 220
    organization closure, 279–282
    participation in board meetings, 160,
    164–165
    position descriptions, 213
    presearch assessments, 212–213
    profiles of desired characteristics, 213
    reference checks, 215
    retirement, 234

    role in human resource matters, 180–181
    roles of, 5, 13, 152, 198–200, 218–222
    search committees, 213–214
    termination of, 235–236
Chief financial officers, 67, 166, 249
Chief operating officers, 201
Churches
    designating two chief executives, 200–201
Clifton, Donald O., 193–194
Closure of organizations, 279–282
Committee chairs, 83
Committee meetings. *See also* Board
meetings; Committees
    developing the agenda, 152
    follow-up, 153
    improving effectiveness of, 151–153
    reference books, 152
    telephone conference calls, 173
Committee reference books, 152
Committees. *See also* Committee meetings;
Executive committees
    appointment to, 83
    audit committee, 249–251
    board chair's role, 62–63
    chairs, 83, 152
    effectiveness of, 81
    former board member assignments, 284
    governance committees, 45, 68, 94–95
    minutes from meetings, 79
    nominating committees, 68, 94–95, 97–98
    nonboard members on committees, 135
    roles of, 6, 83–84, 152
    staff liaisons, 152
    staffing, 84
    traditional committees, 82, 151
Communities
    communication of board activities, 35–39
Compensation. *See also* Salaries
    for board members, 110–113, 184
    for chief executive, 207–211
    performance-based, 209–210
    for staff, 207–211
Conference calls, 173
Conflicts-of-interest, 112, 127–128, 184, 188,
270, 272–274
Consensus determination, 169–170
Consent minutes, 173–174
Constituents
    involvement in work of the board, 130–133
Consultants
    benefits of, 261
    for evaluating board performance, 43–44
    hiring, 260–262

H

Heimovics, Richard D., 219
Herman, Robert D., 219
Human resource issues
  board's role, 179–182

I

Implementation role, 4, 9–11
Inclusive boards, 114
Income sources, 244–246
Intermediate sanctions, 211, 248
Internal Revenue Service
  bylaws requirement for exempt status, 198
  Form 990, 249
  intermediate sanctions, 211, 248
Internet
  access to meeting minutes, 80
  for board information, 174
  for consent minutes, 173–174
IRS. *See* Internal Revenue Service

J

Joint initiatives, 255–259

K

Kanter, Rosabeth Moss, 256–257

L

Large boards. *See also* Size of boards
  examples of, 50
  executive committee policymaking, 50–51
  operations of, 15–17
Leadership styles
  board-centered, 219–222
  decisive, 194
  disciplined, 194–195
  energetic, 196
  ethical, 192–193
  motivators, 192
  organized, 194–195
  persuaders, 192
  servant-leadership, 288
  strengths focused, 193–194
  vision bearers, 191–192
Legal audits, 275–278
Lions Clubs International, 256
Little, Rick, 255

M

Majority votes, 169
Meeting minutes. *See* Minutes from meetings
Meetings. *See* Board meetings; Committee meetings
Members of the board. *See* Board members
Membership organizations
  board representation, 132
  president's role, 197
  selection of board members, 96–99
Mentors, 94, 161, 262–264
Mergers, 281
Merit pay, 209–210
Minutes from meetings
  approval of, 78–79
  committee minutes, 79
  detail of, 78
  electronic access, 80
  executive committees, 59
  format for, 78
  recording "moved, seconded, and carried" motions, 171
  responsibility for, 77
  standing policies manuals, 79
  storage of, 79
Mission
  board's role in, 23–24, 32
  chief executive's role, 32
  establishing policies, 31–32
  evaluating results, 33
  fund-raising policies, 31
  of organization, 119
  strategies for developing resources, 33
Mission statements, 24
Moral owners
  board chair's responsibilities to, 65
  identification of, 35
  involvement in work of the board, 130–133
  of nonprofit boards, 4
"Moved, seconded, and carried" motions, 171
MSC. *See* "Moved, seconded, and carried" motions

N

National Center for Nonprofit Boards. *See* BoardSource
Nepotism, 127, 128
No-vote policy, 184–185, 220
Nominating committees, 68, 94–95, 97–98
Nonmembership organizations
  board representation, 132